CONFES
HEADTEACHER

Ruminations in Lockdown

Hans van Mourik Broekman

LOVE GIVES US EYES: THE VERY FACT OF LOVING MAKES US SEE, CREATES FOR THE LOVING SUBJECT A NEW SPECIES OF EVIDENCE.

-PIERRE ROUSSELOT

CONTENTS

Introduction

This short book was written during the lockdown caused by the Covid-19 pandemic. In the middle of a school year, all schools in the United Kingdom were closed as part of an effort to limit the contagion of the coronavirus. Suddenly, a completely unforeseen event had shut schools. Teachers scrambled to switch their teaching to on-line platforms. Small hub schools were created to look after the children of key workers and those pupils who were vulnerable in a home school setting. Overnight, our bustling campus became an empty and silent park.

The pace of change meant that the pace of innovation needed was very high. No school plans for a pandemic. There was an urgent need to make sure that pupils could continue to learn, continue to be safe, continue to engage with school, continue to be educated.

My colleagues and I threw ourselves into the creation of this new school in a weekend, a school which exists even now only on- line. The lockdown was the necessary condition for me to write this short book. Before the lockdown, I had neither the time, energy, or inclination to write about our school, and certainly not a book of my own ruminations, confessions, critiques, and cerebrations. Nor did it seem necessary in those "normal days" to think about or make notes about the way our school works or does not work. Like any teacher or headteacher, my days were filled with meetings which produced and developed plans, with teaching, mentoring, disciplining, encouraging, and inspiring.

To lead a school is to live a life of what to the outside world must seem a series of iron routines dictated by timetables and school bells. In fact, it is a pretty frantic existence immersed in almost every possible permutation of the human drama. It is rivetingly exciting. A thrill ride for the soul. The lockdown was a sudden immersion into a totally changed experience of school. In my case this experience was one of interiority and reflection. I was no longer around colleagues and pupils for 10 to 12 hours a day. Instead I sat more or less alone in my study pondering when school might re-open. Instead of school bells and exuberant noises of pupils, I clicked into regularly scheduled zoom meetings and spoke to colleagues on the phone.

The pandemic lockdown could therefore best be described as a radically new experience for me. An experience of reality I had not had before and an experience of helpless dependence which headteachers rarely have. Every headteacher I know is trained and encouraged to plan actions, and drive improvement, preferably measurable improvement. But in the form of this nasty virus, a new reality had entered this usual pattern of analysing and pursuing paths and plans of improvement. Here at last we were all, and I especially, confronted by a reality so large that it would never succumb to a new school improvement plan!

This experience of contingency and dependence makes people respond in different ways. Because of the many talented colleagues I work with, I quickly learned that I could add no value to their genius by spending my time supervising their on-line assignments and checking that they responded to pupil concerns quickly. I recognized something which I had sensed before in my 22 years as a headteacher but had always managed to quickly and successfully suppress, namely, that headteachers frequently impede the organic innovation and development of teaching with their faith in their own leadership and action.

As the lockdown wore on and the days inevitably began to flow into each other, I began to read and think about the school in a new way. Its absence had in some sense made it more present to me. I saw the school differently.

In times of change, questions are natural and in a time of total dependence and helplessness in the face of new circumstances one begins to ask challenging questions. What is school for? What does it mean to educate a pupil? What is a teacher? Why do we teach what we teach? Why does school not work for so many children? Why do pupils misbehave? Why did I become a teacher? What do I really want as a headteacher, what desire of my heart impels me to do this work? What makes me joyful in school? What is the source of my wariness about school? Is our school a real community? How well does this school work for pupils?

For some these questions may have been answered months previously in the total of 9 consecutive Ofsted outstanding verdicts on the school over the course of two inspections. Indeed, these "judgments" as they are called, had until the lockdown provided me with a quick assurance that all was indeed well. But in lockdown, my questions led me to a surprising, more complex, and in some sense more fundamental and harsher judgment, especially on myself.

That is why this book has confession in its title. It is the result of an examination not only of our school but also of my conscience as a headteacher. It is not a confession in the sense of a public listing of all my failings before my colleagues and family. They know me well and live every day with my shortcomings, failings and errors. My own reflections on them would not be news to them. The book is a confession in the sense that it is a public communication of this examination of my conscience as a headteacher. It is also a public profession of my beliefs, of what I truly believe about school.

For those who picked up or downloaded this short book in the hope of vicariously luxuriating in the unadulterated account of the misdeeds and foibles of a headteacher, of common room assignations and dirty dealings, I am afraid you will be disappointed.

I did not consult data in writing this book. What follows are thoughts formed in the heart, a confession and articulation of convictions and doubts about the assumptions and motivations which drive the working of our school. This book does not have a bibliography. It is not another call to reform. It is neither quantitative nor qualitative research. It is a personal account and does not reflect the views of anyone associated with Liverpool College, other than myself obviously.

As a statement of belief, the book has antecedents. It has inspirations and influences. I feel I must offer them both as disclaimer and explanation. I am a Roman Catholic Christian and this shapes my view and experience of everything. During the lockdown I was especially inspired by the writing of the late Fr. Luigi Giussani who was a Milanese Catholic priest and high school educator and his friend and frequent collaborator the late Fr. Lorenzo Albacete of New York. Their writings are hardly well known in the English-speaking world but those who do know something about them will immediately see the great extent to which their analysis of education has aided and shaped my examination of what I think and what I do as principal of Liverpool College. Indeed, this book is a response to their inspiration.

I share it not because these ruminations are brilliant and original, but only because they are honest, and, I hope, therefore, compelling.

In writing about education, I make claim only to the particular experience that is my own, in a particular school, Liverpool College, in a particular place, at this particular time. I do so in the belief that the many books and articles that I have read about education which purported to be universal in their application were, upon closer inspection, neither universal nor applicable. When we speak of something as mysterious as education or as complex as school, the particular is perhaps all we can speak about, and even then, with great difficulty and uncertainty.

Because so much of what is attempted in school is mandated, directed, or encouraged by institutions and people outside of the school who are charged with ensuring the development of a "system of education", thoughts, beliefs, doubts, and critiques about what happens in our school are to some extent critiques and doubts about the "system" and by extension about what is likely happening in other schools. The particular in schools is always related to larger spheres, larger questions, larger influences, larger purposes.

This confession should not be interpreted as a consciousness of collective failure or reproach to anyone. It is precisely because of the talents and abilities of my colleagues, pupils and parents, that I have been able to think beyond the way the school is now. They are the inspiration for this book.

At the time of writing, there is understandable speculation about when schools in the United

Kingdom will open again. That they will one day open again is the only certainty. There will be urgency and demand to return to the situation BC (before Coronavirus) as soon as possible. The premise of this book is that every new beginning is also a reimagining, with an openness to all the possibilities and all the factors of reality. Schools after Coronavirus and Covid-19 will not be like schools before corona. The intense experience of briefly not being a school, as we understood that term, will help us become a better one.

Chapter 1

EDUCATION

What Does Our School Think It Is Doing?

Singers sing. Orchestras make music. Football teams play football. Governments govern. But what do schools do? Or perhaps: What do schools think they are doing? How does a school understand itself?

There are plenty of institutions with mission or intent statements which employ more than one verb to describe their activity. Most have a limited number of activities which define what they do. A university, for example, usually understands itself as engaging in two core actions: research and teaching. Hospitals, whatever their mission statements ultimate understand that they diagnose and treat disease. At Jaguar Land Rover, down the road in nearby Halewood, they know that they design and build cars.

Schools, our own included, I believe struggle with this. Attempts to simplify the school's understanding of itself seem doomed to failure. Schools struggle to limit the number of verbs they associate with themselves. It is as difficult for a school to list all the verbs that describe its activity as it would be for a family to do so. All of us would struggle to write a mission statement for our families, and if we did, it would look a lot like the mission statement of a school!

The best explanation for why this is so is that schools are ultimately about the entirety of the human experience, just like families are. Every school is literally a school of life, imaging and containing within itself all the drama and mystery of the human condition.

But rather than just saying that, which would perhaps frighten us, and would certainly utterly perplex us, there are a number of verbs which are inevitably bandied about when we talk about the ineffable activity of school. These are verbs which express what we think the school is doing. Teach, nurture, inspire, guide, counsel, develop, learn, train, safeguard, school (as a verb), and educate.

If we were honest and took account of the proportion of time we all spend on various activities within school we would have to add verbs like feed, supervise, compete. The particulars of a day in which 1800 people are fed in 90 minutes, 300 lessons are taught, and where innumerable "chats", encouragements, communications, corrections, detentions, exchanges and interactions take place are not meant to be considered in isolation. Our self-understanding, of course, combines all these activities toward an over-arching goal, a sort of summation towards which all this activity tends, a sum which is greater than the verbs. These verbs are not undertaken for themselves but are intended to contribute in every possible way to the experience of school which in turn is seeking to …..do what exactly? Most of us would use the verb educate to describe this totality and when we try to explain what that is we use phrases like: "maximising human potential", or "nurturing and inspiring young people to grow, to develop, to become independent". The question then begs to be asked: Develop to what? Independent from what?

Under further self-questioning and the onslaught of existential disorientation (easily avoided in the hectic life of the school day), we are quickly clinging ever more strenuously to the nearest cliché. We educate for life, for freedom. We struggle to verbalize our self-understanding because we know that we are not entirely sure but we are certain that we do not only train our pupils in particular skills. We do not only transfer particular knowledge or even a set of propositions or hypotheses. Somehow, although we cannot describe it, our school's self- understanding is always that it is doing more than that. We are forming people, we might say. We are changing lives, we might add. We are creating the much desired "independent learner".

A colleague and I fell into this dizzying abyss once and quickly recovered ourselves. We admitted we could not say exactly what education was, but we could definitely see whether or not our efforts to educate were working or not through our interactions with our pupils.

In our defense, I would make two observations about our rather perplexed conclusion. At least we instinctively understood that the effect of a successful education would not be primarily or only revealed in academic ability or performance. Ours was a holistic view of the person's educational journey. Secondly, we expressed, perhaps haltingly, that education concerns the totality of the human person, something which is by no means obvious to all. We knew that the effect of a school as per the education it provides would be seen in the life of a person, even if we could not verbalize what this effect would be or the process by which it occurs. I do not remember whether we finished our chat by telling each other that we were in front of a great mystery. I do not think we allowed ourselves that thought as we were simultaneously trying to supervise the lunch line.

I am not aware of any school which says it trains its pupils or says it schools them. I train my dog. I also helped to potty train my children. We train nurses, doctors, and (more on this later) teachers. Schools tend not to use the word training. Somehow the idea of "training for life" smacks of a reform school or borstal. "Schooling" is also avoided. It has the slightly disreputable whiff of chalk dust and corporal punishment on it. We call ourselves educators not trainers. We aim to do well in the Ofsted judgment: quality of education. There is no Ofsted judgment in schools for quality of training, which we associate with the acquisition of narrowly defined technical skills.

Most teachers and pupils have been lectured on the meaning of the word education and its etymology from the Latin "educere", to lead out. This is usually favourably contrasted with the etymology of training from the Latin "trahere", to drag out. Our working assumption, to the extent that we consider the matter, is that we are educators educating, although what this means remains for us ineffable, undefined, and to a certain sense unscrutinised. We educate, but we are not able to say what that is.

Perhaps it is possible to do something very well when you do not know what you are doing. Mo Salah probably does not theorize about scoring goals, he shoots. I am reminded of the US Supreme Court judge who was asked to rule on a definition of the word obscene. He claimed he could not give one but this did not matter as he would know something was obscene when he saw it.

Our lives as educators are not like an instinctive technical skill such as shooting at goal. Our avoidance of this question of exactly what we are doing in school is an excellent example of the unexamined lives we are all to a certain extent living. It is not that we do not know what to do in our school. For years, former pupils have returned to thank us for the excellent education they received from us. They are the true measure of our success, and nothing gives more joy than hearing this sort of acknowledgment from someone who attended our school. Their testimony encourages us. We are getting it right. Next time this happens, however, I hope I have the presence of mind to ask them what they mean when they say we educated them well. In my experience, these statements from pupils are not only about the way we helped them achieve academic success or entry to a course or employment. They are referring to a gratitude for help in a wider development of their persons-social, intellectual, moral, personal, spiritual, aesthetic, physical. Their own understanding of this reality in their lives is seemingly certain but too complicated to fully explain. They are in some sense thanking us for developing their whole selves.

But our failure to enunciate a clear definition of education does not only affect our ability to recognize what we are doing right and why we are doing it right. Our reluctance to delve deeply into the fundamental dynamic of education shapes the kind of school our pupils attend in very profound ways. It makes us more likely to confuse the contingent elements of school with the necessary ones.

We are, if we are ignorant or sloppy in our understanding of what education actually is and how it works, more likely to fill our days and our school with stuff that is not important. In this sense, absent clarity, we are like a business that is not able to describe its core activity to a visitor in 25 words or less.

The best definition of education I have come across is from an Austrian theologian. Andreas Jungmann wrote that education is "the introduction of the person into reality in all its factors." Introduction in German has the actual sense of guiding someone into something, almost by the hand. An education is that process which guides the human person into an encounter with reality in all its factors. It draws the person out, as in the original sense of "educere", guiding the person out to an engagement with all of reality, all that is not "I". It is a movement of the person toward an embrace of reality, in all its factors.

I am increasingly conscious that it is a typical error of schools to seek to understand and even develop education from the perspective of what the educators do rather than from the perspective of what those being educated, in our case our pupils, experience. From the perspective of the pupil, what she experiences in education as distinct from schooling and training, is the engagement of her freedom. An education is an invitation to a person to exercise freedom during the introduction to reality. As a school, we tend to focus on all the things we can do to engage a person in this journey. This book is an attempt to focus on the needs and desires of a person who is being educated, whose freedom must be provoked or risked if we want to educate.

We experience education when our freedom is engaged and in play, when our "I", our self is able to grapple with reality. When we do not experience this appeal to our "I" during our learning, this appeal to our freedom, we do not experience education, we experience training.

This is why training can be very dull and education is always exciting. Education contains the factor of human freedom and is therefore a risky and dangerous activity with a high rate of failure. It is always open to new experiences, new possibilities, new intimations and invitations. It is dangerous because the risk when we engage someone's freedom is that they reject the activity and the content of what is being offered and proposed for learning. There is no guarantee of success in education.

If schools want to educate rather than train, they should focus on how an introduction to the totality of reality can engage a person's freedom. We tend to think that schools should be "effective" in the sense that the activity of a school should lead to the communication and integration of knowledge and the development of certain skills or habits. The standard of success we set is that this should happen 100% of the time for 100% of our pupils. I am certain that in any classroom where 100% of the pupils learn 100% of the stuff they are supposed to, no education occurs, only training. We have to accept that education, when it engages the freedom of a human person is a high-risk, high -reward activity where failure at any particular moment is almost as common as success.

Chapter 2

LEARNING

Persons Here, Persons There, Persons Absolutely Everywhere

In 1974 Thomas Nagel published his influential philosophy paper entitled "What is it like to be a bat?" In the essay, Nagel conducts a thought experiment. If it were possible to know from our human perspective everything that was happening in the brain or, even more widely, the consciousness of a bat, would it be possible to know what it is like to be a bat? Nagel answered no. Even with total information about every aspect of the bat, we would not be able to know what it is like to be a bat. Only a bat would know that, only THE bat would know that.

I am certain I have simplified the mind-consciousness controversies which flow from Nagel's essay. There are many brilliant people who disagree vehemently with Nagel. I sometimes suspect these people have somehow found work at Ofsted.

I think of Nagel and his bat often when I enter a classroom either to teach or to watch others teach. It is of course vitally important to recognize who is sitting behind these desks in our classrooms. We take attendance and read out names. We are conscious of the individuality of those names. We anticipate the way their background and stories, the way even their personalities and actions have in the past and will probably today influence our teaching and the culture in the class. Some of the names on the register are starred or coloured to help us remember a need these pupils bring to our classroom. Sometimes we can even click through and see the data, which clearly reveals these needs. And then we begin. To teach. They hopefully begin to learn. What are we thinking when we do this? What do we actually think we are doing? How are we going about this?

I suspect that everything we have been taught about this process in our teacher training, in our CPD, in our reading of the popular teaching books like <u>Make it Stick</u>, and in so called "best practice", is based on a reduction, a reduction of the pupil, a reduction of ourselves. We have set aside Nagel's conclusion which might have served as a warning that we could never know what it is like to be someone else, and quickly availed ourselves of a working hypothesis about our pupils which empowers us to believe that we can understand and direct what is happening in a classroom containing more than 30 persons.

The first reduction is the name learner. The fashion for this is enormous at the moment. Pupils, having forfeited upon entry through the gates of our school the name of person, are now not even pupils. They are now "learners". It is all about the learners. We have all ingested this definition of learning which neuroscience presents. For some, ingestion has already proceeded to digestion. Policy makers, researchers, and headteachers are all captivated by the idea that brain science will ultimately provide the insights which will unlock learning itself and by extension teaching itself. True learning produces knowledge. Knowledge is a permanent change in the brain. There you have it. It is impossible to argue with the biology of this statement. From it flow the various learning theories: behaviourism, constructivism, growth mindset et cetera. You can Google all 15 of them presented in tidy lists. The various learning theories are all backed by an appeal to the provisional and tentative conclusions of neuroscience. The idea that our work in schools could be so adjusted as to ensure desirable changes in the brain is very attractive because it would solve forever the ancient question asked of Socrates in Plato's Gorgias: "How does a person learn something they did not know before?"

This reduction is immensely attractive for a number of reasons. What Plato in <u>Gorgias</u> concludes is an almost ineffable process shrouded in mystery and constituted of incomprehensible subtlety and complexity, now becomes a clearly understood biological process. John Locke's dream of a tabula rasa has finally entered school, backed up by a much-improved understanding of neurons bouncing around frantically in the 30 little heads in front of you. We have in fact unlocked a secret of human development and learning.

The other attraction is that this reductive, functional and materialist view of the child in your classroom makes the problem of all the children who are not learning something which can be addressed. Headteachers love that. Instead of a plaintive prayer and appeal to patience for the transformation of these children, we now have a fairly mechanistic view, a scientifically supported pedagogy, which will enable us to begin to address the problem of pupils who are not learning well enough immediately.

This is a further reduction. Not only has a person become a learner, a neuron receptacle, but pedagogical techniques can actually shape and direct that neuron receptacle.

The importers of neuroscience into education would themselves dismiss my description of their work as a gross oversimplification, a reduction. It is incontrovertible that an understanding of the biology of the brain can help us teach better, and helps us to understand why so many people struggle to learn.

But ultimately, I am totally unpersuaded that this is, today, the most fruitful way to think about schools, pupils or learning. No matter how much the materialist neuroscientists and pedagogues try to persuade me, I find their enthusiasm does not spur any passion in me. I am pretty sure it does not spur any passion in our pupils either having seen the bored and blank expression on their faces when concepts like these are explained to them by me and other dutiful educators, perhaps in the vain hope that pupils, I mean learners, will work along with this materialist conception of themselves and thus improve their "learning" and develop a "growth mindset".

It is impossible for anyone to accept as true something about themselves which does not in any way comport with or even contradicts their actual experience. This is especially true in a young person who has not yet developed the power to delude oneself in which adults excel. Indeed, as the great French philosopher Jean Guitton said, "reasonable is the word we use to describe a person who submits her reason to the scrutiny of her experience." Whilst we as educators do not always follow this advice, in my experience, persons, I mean pupils, I mean learners, most definitely are reasonable and they find this materialist understanding of themselves does not comport with their experience, the only criterion of judgment which a reasonable person will use.

My experience tells me that persons are not reducible to pupils or to learners. There is in every person an irreducibly mysterious "I". I can describe and enumerate for a child their motivation, their background, their attachment trauma, their learning style, their SEND need, their anxiety, their evolutionary biology, their neurons. I can, as schools often do, give a complete dossier of knowledge to the child explaining who they are, and the child will still say: "But I love Jimmy." That "I" has infinite desires which our finite philosophy and neuroscience cannot satisfy. The reality of a life in school has taught me that the human species has biologically and materially evolved to have desires which biology and the material world can neither explain nor satisfy. That "I" does not find that my description of the reasonable, the possible, the sensible, the profitable, the prudent or the scientifically demonstrable and verifiable, satisfies the desires of its heart.

I have observed, in the melee and maelstrom that constitutes school life and culture, that our materialist model of the child has, unfortunately, and despite our own experience and reason, begun to affect the way we talk with them and about them, leading to occasional rage and frustration on both our and their sides.

When a child says "I," we seem to have trained ourselves to deconstruct and therefore reduce that "I", to explain even the irreducible "I" to ourselves. We hear in that "I" a biological "I", an evolutionary "I", a sociological "I", a psychological "I", a cognitive "I", an emotional "I", a pedagogical "I", even an unreasonable "I".

I have been pondering why it is that we think we can understand our pupils, I mean learners, when it is so obvious that we do not understand ourselves. I think it may be because, being professionals, people turn to us for answers, for a proposed course of action, for a diagnosis of some sort. This is particularly true in the case of a pupil who is not learning or finds it difficult to learn. In some cases there are clear and scientifically verifiable reasons why a child is not learning. It is always a great gift when a school can help a child understand why she struggles to learn through the application of verifiable scientific methods.

But in my experience, there are as many or even more cases of pupils struggling in school where neuroscience, psychology, and sociology offer absolutely no solace, no relief and no diagnosis of note. It turns out that we are seemingly powerless, despite our various reductions of the person in front of us, to solve the riddle that that person is to themselves. But it never seems to stop schools from developing a plan of action.

From time to time, these plans have a real effect. I do not think that is because the science or research behind them is particularly useful or even helpful. The desire to perform a reduction of the individual person using scientific terms is relatively new in schools and seems predicated on the idea that science "works" and that teachers must not only "cure" their pupils but also give a plausible diagnosis, usually couched in terms of a neurological, emotional, social or psychological pathology.

The most common disease or pathology in school is not flu or colds but a mild and lazy nihilism and apathy caused in part by the failure of school to make its activity meaningful to some pupils. No one ever makes that diagnosis and the "cure" for this ennui cannot be sought through the reduction of the totality of the person. I have noticed that some colleagues are able to engage the full "I" of the pupil, without reduction. They do not treat the pupil as a pupil, or even a learner. The pupil experiences their interaction with these colleagues as what I can only describe as the encounter with a real "mensch". These colleagues do not seek to make a reductive diagnosis but instead work from a different assumption, an assumption of freedom and responsibility, of the irreducible dignity and mystery of the person. Their approach begins with an appeal to the complexity that is an "I", a person, whose freedom can respond to an invitation, who can be called to a full encounter with reality, who must be "dealt with" in a totally unreduced way. They refuse to talk to pupils as if we in the teaching profession are in possession of a knowledge which we will drip feed over their 14 years with us until all there is to know about themselves is understood by them as we believe it already is by us.

Our understanding of our learners is a conscious decision. We can choose to reduce them and to valorise our supposed knowledge and understanding. We can, in short, disagree with Nagel and believe that we can know what it is like to be someone else. Or we can bring to them what we can and do know whilst always remembering that our learners are involved in a terrible and often lonely struggle, a struggle to make sense of the mystery of their own deepest desires. We do not have the answers to that mystery, and even if we did, they would not help because the pupil is not the object but the subject of our school, of our activity. They are the protagonists of the story of the school. They themselves will need to explore their own irreducible "I" and their own desires of their hearts, their own experience.

If we acknowledged the challenge of that journey for them and pointed out their freedom to respond to the challenges the journey throws up, they might listen to us more attentively.

Chapter 3

TEACHING

To Be a Teacher

I have frequently and publicly confessed that I am not a trained teacher. I am therefore always conscious of an inferiority. But I did try during my career to make up for this deficiency. For a few years, while teaching full time, I took graduate courses in educational leadership at a university in Baltimore in the United States. I probably do not give enough credit to these courses for teaching me things which underpin my practice and understanding today.

The best part of these courses, like the best part of my own experience of school, were the teachers, the professors. I remember one would-be Socrates who was asked by a perceptive classmate which subject he had taught before becoming a professor of education. This was done in the form of the question: "What did you teach before you became a professor?" His answer was: "I taught kids."

His answer was effective at several levels. It provoked some thought, always a good thing in a teacher. It also allowed him to score a cheap point, affirming a sort of politically correct way of self-understanding, that the object of school education is a child and that he was a teacher of stupendous holistic insight as opposed to the feeble minds and withered hearts found everywhere in the profession.

But his answer also revealed a truth that I have come to appreciate. The verb to teach does have this amazing property of being able to take as its object both human persons and knowledge. In our school, like many others, we have recently focused more on knowledge as the object of our teaching. Many teachers' self-understanding is that their primary activity is imparting new knowledge to their pupils. In this model of teaching, the teacher plans and directs activity which creates knowledge in a pupil. When compelled to reflect on how exactly this is done, teachers themselves tend to suggest that the evidence based-pedagogical strategies they deploy make this happen consistently. In a culture where teachers understand their work in this way, my former professor would not last a second because he would be suspected of being too child focused and insufficiently content focused. He would be deemed to be suspiciously unenthusiastic about teaching techniques and strategies and far too confident in the power of his personality. At interview his utterances, however brilliant he himself conceived them to be, would mean he would not progress to the next round.

Is there any good reason, from our experience, for teachers' current certainty about what teaching, especially good teaching, looks like? If good teaching is so clearly recognized and understood, why is it so difficult and why does so much teaching have very little impact on the lives of students? In short, if we have such a clear picture of teaching, why do so many pupils fail? It seems to me that if learning is a mysterious process, teaching may be even more so. It is very difficult to unpick exactly what the essence of the work of a great teacher is. After reading the personal educational philosophies of many teaching candidates and listening to teachers' reflections on what they do, it is clear to me that teachers themselves, while professing to know what great teaching looks like, struggle to describe certain dimensions of their activity.

Teachers' self-understanding as imparters of knowledge means they commonly conceive of themselves as technicians of cognition, therapists of neurons who through "sessions" commonly referred to as "lessons" manipulate and activate the cognitive abilities of learners. Using the active engagement of the pupil, repetition and practice, carefully crafted tasks and challenges, and the considered and focused application of teaching strategies, the teacher activates the learner to obtain knowledge, new knowledge, which can be recalled, and which then enables an ability to absorb or master more new knowledge even more quickly, in a kind of virtuous circle of filling up the brain.

Who could dispute this? It is like arguing that the sea does not have salt or the earth is flat. Of course, this self-understanding "works" so far as it goes. Which, if we examine our own experience, is not very far. It is not that great teachers are not effective cognition technicians, it is just that great teachers, in our own experience, seem to do a lot more than lead the activity which ensures we learn ever more complex content. I am not sure we remember our favourite or most influential and transformational teacher because they were most effective in getting us to learn material. We tend to describe our best teacher, instead, using words like inspirational, motivational, life-changing.

My own suspicion, based on my experience as a pupil and student and my reflection on the experience of seeing hundreds of teachers teach, is that the self-understanding of a teacher as a cognition technician is an incomplete and inaccurate picture or a reduction of what the teacher actually does. Truly effective teaching is more exciting, difficult, demanding and mysterious than the facilitation of the absorption of knowledge. The teacher is a unique and irreducible embodiment of the adventure, impact and reward of learning. Their person, their "I" is an essential ingredient in a process which combines several factors and cannot be reduced to a transfer of knowledge only.

Teaching is an encounter, a meeting between persons who bring unique desires, hopes, fears and experiences into the encounter. Effective teaching occurs when the teacher's invitation to the pupil resonates with the freedom of the pupil to engage. A teacher achieves this engagement of a pupil not only through a strategic and tactical pedagogical communication, as suggested in our current mechanistic self-understanding of teaching and learning, but also through a communication of themselves, a communication in the form of the person of the teacher. Effective teachers embody for the pupil a passion for and conviction about the meaning of the subject they teach. This passion and conviction are rooted in the impact that the meaning of the subject and the adventure of learning has exerted in their own person. This personal and unique communication of passion and conviction is the gift of the teacher to the pupil. It is this communication of the teacher's person which is the essential ingredient in great teaching. In the encounter between teacher and pupil, the teacher is reporting from a place beyond what the pupil already knows and bringing to the pupil a conviction about the value and meaning of life as experienced in the engagement with the subject. This report becomes an invitation to learn because the teacher's very person proposes to the pupil a compelling and attractive vision of what lies beyond the subject, of the next step in learning and in life, and the step after that, and the step after that.

Just as my old professor said "I teach kids", it can therefore also be said that a teacher should be able to say: "Children learn me." Because education is an introduction to aspects of reality not yet known to us, experienced by us, or understood by us, we need a guide who invites us to pursue the purpose of our engagement with it. This can only be done by a person because it is only through a person that the impact and value and meaning of the learning of the subject can be revealed to another person. It is in the encounter with the person of the teacher that the possibility, potential, and value of learning is suddenly revealed and realized. We commonly refer to this process as the teacher motivating or inspiring the pupil. When we think about the great teachers we have experienced, it is this gift of themselves in the process of invitation and inspiration which we remember, not the ability to communicate or transfer knowledge.

Some might say this way of describing teaching is an impractical pipe dream because the self-understanding of the teacher and of teaching we are describing is too complex and vague. Some will argue that it is not possible to train a person to act out of such a self-understanding. They would say that very few people could teach with a full awareness and deployment of all these factors. As such, it might be argued, it is not "realistic" to ask each of the 500.000 full time teachers in the country to view themselves in this way, day in day out, lesson after lesson. I am reminded of the comments of Prime Minister Johnson's closest advisor Dominic Cummings that education and specifically teaching should be more like Tesco: doing the basics well, less innovation, more systemization, tighter routines, more efficiency.

This dream Mr. Cummings dreams is one of an unfailing standard and method of depersonalized teaching which consistently unlocks the learning capacity of any child no matter who is teaching them. It removes the complex and to some extent uncontrollable presence of a person with insights, creative impulses, failings, moods, opinions, views, motivations, personal experiences and personal needs from the act of teaching and replaces this person with a trained clinician who can deploy effective strategies without involving their person. By removing the person of the teacher as the essential ingredient of effective teaching, Mr. Cummings promotes a model of teaching which removes the need to find, develop, recruit, retain and inspire people who are committed to the development of a demanding self- understanding and a requirement to engage the whole of one's person, experiences, hopes, dreams, desires, passions and convictions as a teacher. His reduced understanding of the effective teacher probably appeals to many who want to live out a "career" rather than pursue a vocation. The Cummings view positively affirms the idea that a teacher should not be expected to commit their person to their teaching.

This reduced view and self-understanding of teaching has opened up the profession to many people who need a job and who may not have any very strong conviction or passion to give or communicate. It has enabled teaching to present itself as a career choice which a "professional" might wish to make, including opportunities to progress, and competitive renumeration. It has not made teachers happier or teaching more popular. I keep being emailed the results of studies which show there is a teacher recruitment crisis and that one in five teachers want to leave the profession, preferably as soon as possible.

My own suspicion about the causes of this unpopularity of teaching is that our reduced view of teaching may mean we have falsely advertised what it takes to be a great teacher. This may have led us to recruit people who, when they actually begin to teach, realize that while they are meeting all the checklist requirements of effective teaching nevertheless derive no satisfaction from their work because their heart is just not in it. For such a person, teaching is a nightmare job because the structure of the activity of teaching and learning, the desires and demands of pupils and the examples of colleagues with a much-expanded self-understanding of being a teacher all combine to produce feelings of inferiority and alienation. What had been presented as a profession that one could harmlessly pursue, in the manner that one might be a lawyer or accountant, turns out to require the gift of oneself and an endless number of encounters with lots of demanding young people in a very personal and non-socially and emotionally-distanced way. We owe it to the profession and to those considering it to paint an accurate picture of what a great teacher does and to recruit only those who are prepared to try it out on this basis.

From the perspective of the pupil, our reduced self-understanding of teaching and effective teachers has even more profound consequences. Because our current self-understanding as teachers glorifies teaching techniques over the engagement of our person, pupils are subjected in school to a tremendous sameness. It is difficult to describe how similar their experiences are in each lesson. It is only when you follow a pupil around for a whole day, which teachers themselves cannot do, that you can experience what our reduced view of the teacher has wrought for them. In classroom after classroom, the pedagogy is similar, and because the teachers all operate on the basis of "evidence-based" teaching strategies, similar strategies and routines are used everywhere. In the beginning of my career I stumbled across examples of teaching that were highly eccentric, original, personal, and perhaps less than 100% effective for "cognition transfer" or learning as defined by a permanent change in the brain. They were however highly effective in eliciting enthusiasm, desire, passion, conviction and motivation in pupils to engage with the adventure of learning. The unique encounter with the person of their teacher produced for many pupils an attraction to the material studied and a desire to engage. Now, in perfectly planned and pedagogically correct lessons, I frequently want to shout over the heads of the pupils towards my teaching colleagues: "Just be you! Please!" Pupils experience this sameness when the person of the teacher is not present, not engaged. For them, there is in such lessons no true encounter, no invitation, no guide.

How did we as a profession get to this point of accepting a self-understanding of teaching that does not coincide with our own experience? The reduction and depersonalization of teaching and the alienation of teachers is bred during teacher training. Here bright young people are taught or trained in the "the way to teach". They do not have the vocabulary or experience to express their doubts about the disembodied theory of teaching being presented. In order to pass, they must swallow this desiccated vision of teaching whole. They are constantly reminded that they are joining a profession, and this is how it is done. They are trained in accountability and in the systematic communication of curricular content, not encouraged to use their imagination to communicate something of their own experience of the adventure of learning. The quality of reflection on the teacher's art or vocation is limited and constrained by mechanistic pedagogical theories and constant appeals to evidence and research which do not usually allow for an examination of the desire of the heart to teach. In fact, teaching is not presented as a vocation or an art but as a skill of communicating content which leads to membership of a profession as represented by acronyms like NQT, QTS and PGCE. This is training after all, not education. Reflection, to the extent that it occurs or is encouraged, means reflection on practice already established, on best practice, not on how practice can be renewed or on the requirement to develop my own person in order to become a great teacher.

After this year of indoctrination, some newly qualified teachers are lucky enough to get a job in a school where some greater or deeper vision of teaching survives, perhaps a faith school or a school where the leadership has effectively fought a rear- guard action, carving out a space for differences between and among teachers and their teaching. Here teachers cling like shipwrecks to a vision of themselves as self-giving educators rather than cognition technicians. They stay in touch with their vocation, their passion, their own convictions. Surrounded by some transformational teachers, the newly qualified observe that these inspirational experienced colleagues are not just technicians of cognition and that they immediately and decisively abandon anything which prevents them from embodying and communicating their personal passion for the drama and meaning of education.

It is good that such places and such teachers exist. It turns out that the human species needs more than the deliberate and systematic stimulation of cognition toward the formation of new knowledge. We need guides who are themselves transformed by the way learning transformed their experience of life and of reality, to show us in their person what is possible for us.

Chapter 4

CURRICULUM

The Battle Over Our Introduction To Reality

Curriculum is in vogue. After years of believing that school accountability and school governance and leadership structure were the essential ingredients to improving the education of young people, policymakers have now concluded something which was apparent to many people who work in schools. The curriculum matters. Credit goes to Ms. Spielman, the head of the inspectorate, for recognizing this and for changing the way the regulator inspects curricula in schools.

There is now a great emphasis on curriculum, its development, its structure, content, and depth. It is difficult to make a case that the words "broad and balanced" have not penetrated every school in England as the way to test if a curriculum design is actually meeting its most basic requirements. The idea seems to be that a broad, balanced and especially challenging curriculum is required for all. This curriculum, it is hoped, will ensure that the pupil will be ready for the "next step" in their education and life.

It is fruitless to argue with this, or to make a case that some things are not as balanced as Ms. Spielman wishes they were. We can have endless arguments about what exactly should be in the curriculum. I suspect that everyone accepts that as a country and as a school, we just have to keep thinking deeply about this and make the changes which occur to us. While there is no perfect curriculum just as there is no perfect husband or wife, it is important that we have these arguments about the subjects and content incorporated in the curriculum because it is clear that school curricula not only reflect the assumption and beliefs of a particular country or school but also have a direct impact on the kind of society we become. I think, for example, that the fact that geography is not a specific subject taught in schools in the United States may have something to do with the failure of about 25% of the US population to point to the area designated as Asia on a globe when asked to do so at the time of high school graduation. Such ignorance has real life impact. Similarly, in the Northwest of England only about 15% of boys pass a GCSE in a foreign language. I am certain that such curricular distortions have real life economic, political and cultural consequences. But my purpose is not to make a case for particular curricular content but rather to plead for a new way of looking at the curriculum and how we deliver it.

It would be hard to devise a system of schooling more capable of deadening the love of learning and natural curiosity of children than the implementation of the curriculum in an English school. Indeed, it is a testimony of the native genius and resilience of the English psyche, the power of the Holy Spirt and the personalities of teachers that a significant minority of the population survives 14 years of school with a desire and an ability to keep learning more. Even more amazing are the many children who retain a significant zest for life and exploration throughout their experience of the curriculum. In our school, I have the chance to compare enthusiasm for learning in reception pupils, aged 4, with the enthusiasm commonly on display in Year 10. It is not only developmental and age-related differences which explain the slow extinguishing of enthusiasm for learning in so many pupils over time in school. It is directly related to the way we have constructed, understood, and developed our curriculum.

What can be more depressing than the phrase so often heard in almost every classroom. "You do not need to know that," or its corollary, "Make sure you get this down on the exam"? It is an absolute refrain of school life. I would say it is the lesson English schools teach best. Learn what you need to and no more.

I once heard an English teacher explain to a child why the poems the class were compelled to study were so boring. During my visit to this English lesson, thumbing through the anthology of poems being studied I was sympathetic to the boy (and it is always a boy) who rather like little Oliver had dared to question the measly distribution of poetic gruel which was destined to be his lot for two years of study. The teacher pointed out that the purpose of the poetry selection in the specification for the exam was not to introduce pupils to the best possible poems, or even the most famous ones, or the ones people had liked throughout history or found most meaningful, but instead to include poems which could be thematically compared with others in order to fit the mark scheme and provide an opportunity for desired skills to be displayed in an exam. Upon returning to my study, I thought long and hard about reporting the exam board to the safeguarding team for suspected child abuse.

Even in an art classroom, one is struck by the constraints imposed on creativity and even beauty by the need to create something that can be measured using skills that can be demonstrated and verified, ultimately according to mark schemes and assessed skills. In science lessons it is quite usual to hear a teacher say: "You have to know what this is but you are not ready to understand the entire explanation of this until later."

This is the country that completely fetishizes examinations, to the point where no nationwide psychiatric intervention or exorcism is any longer possible. We all, our school included, need a miracle.

This fetish has overwhelmed, subverted and perverted any healthy understanding of curriculum and thus any hope that the recent emphasis on curriculum will lead to a rebirth of sound learning. As a country we are determined, quite rightly, to invite and challenge our children to learn as much of what we think is important as possible. In order to assure ourselves that this is in fact happening, we have alighted on exams are our preferred tool for providing this assurance. Exams and qualifications, assessment and data appear to have the benefit of being meritocratic and objective, unable to be manipulated. They lead to results, which we associate with accountability. As we make the examinations more difficult, we can be further assured that our children are learning more and more. Marxist pedagogues have correctly identified the function of examinations in explaining inequalities, a means of justifying both public investment and driving a Sisyphean nightmare of improvement and learning. Particularly pathetic is the belief than an emphasis on STEM subjects will allow us to compete better economically in the world. The idea which drives so much curricular development, namely, that a child slaving to reach expected levels on SATS or being tutored to achieve a 4 in mathematics is somehow a soldier enlisted in a global economic war where higher levels of numeracy are the key to victory would be ridiculous if it were not the stated ministerial intention in curriculum reform.

But, these are the easy observations about how undue influences such as examinations have shaped our entire approach to curriculum and left many of our pupils bored, distracted, and somewhat less than enthusiastic about learning in school. I am not interested in advocating for a change to our pathetic reliance on exams which strikes me as shouting into a cultural headwind of hurricane strength. My interest is in how our definition of truth and reason has created a curriculum which may be broad, balanced and challenging and at the same time without any meaning for the person engaged in it.

And learning is about meaning. The human person enters an engagement with a curriculum as a totality, as a total "I", not as a cartesian rationalist with brain and desire separated. Human curiosity about the world is insatiable. It is the one incurable addiction we all share. What is outside us appears to us a mystery to be solved, a reality to be absorbed. Our original position before it all is wonder. Why leads to why leads to why, in an endless attempt to make sense of reality so that one can make sense of oneself. This is how and why we learn anything and everything, and, as every parent knows, the more the "I" engages with this introduction to reality in all its factors, the deeper our questions go, until, they reach the unanswerable.

This is the structure of reality as a human being experiences it. Reality comes to us as a sign to something else, something beyond itself. This property of reality as being sign is what leads us to experience something as significant, as meaningful. Most teachers and pupils would agree, for example, that if I learn about Tudor England but am not able to explore how this period of time shapes my society, its art, its politics and its self-understanding today, and how events then have percolated into my own life, I am unlikely to find any meaning in Tudor England.

Our search for meaning is even stronger than the above example might indicate. When studying any history, we find that questions arise about the meaning of history itself. Is there causation in the world, in the universe? Does the past matter? To what extent are we able to be "impartial"? Where will history end? Is history a lesson or a warning? Why do people study history?

In the English school curriculum, we do not want to place content inside a quest for meaning and therefore we systematically present subjects outside of larger contexts or questions. In the case of history, we teach it in order to make our pupils good historians not in order to understand the meaning of history.

The same approach is true in every other subject we teach. Our curriculum is structured as a narrow stepladder to university or employment level content. Content and skills are included so that they can lead to the absorption of more and more complex content, not so that a pupil can explore the meaning of the content in relation to the whole of reality. In history this means that our courses avoid "historical surveys" or narrative sweep over longer periods. We focus instead on discreet and totally unrelated periods for intensive study. We do this because we do not believe that history itself has meaning. The point we want to make to pupils is that history is a verb, a human activity, a skill that can be applied. The structure or the meaning of the content matters not.

Now imagine if you were engaged on a daily basis in a curriculum that had deliberately built this wall around itself. A curriculum which was delineated and articulated by boundaries, borders, topics, modules, measurable outcomes and measurable impacts. A curriculum not focused on meaning but on reality only in so far as that reality can be demonstrated through a verifiable and measurable processes. A curriculum presented to you not as an introduction, an invitation to go deeper but as a totality to be accepted as demonstrated truth. A curriculum which pointed to itself as a skill. As a practical matter you would accept this as necessary up to a point. Everyone understands that schools make choices about the content through which they intend to introduce you to the totality of reality.

But as a person you could not passionately engage with something that is not significant in the sense of pointing beyond itself to deeper and further reality and thus to the search to make sense of yourself. This is why the words "you do not need to know that" are so deadening. This is why kids, after the age of 13, are accused in every school of being mere passive sponges, bored even in relationship education lessons! This is why teachers struggle to keep order in secondary schools and why so many children feel apathetic about school. This is why true curiosity in school is so often, over time, drained out of a kid. The curriculum is not structured as an exploration of the human condition. We have made the curriculum a two-dimensional fact, limited it to what is already demonstrated and verified, and failed to incorporate any open-ended search for the meaning and significance of its content. The human being, if not sufficiently resilient or encouraged elsewhere to keep seeking this meaning, will eventually submit to the flatness of this limited education. This leads to much depression, anxiety, apathy and poor behaviour.

The meaning we give something will always have an element of subjectivity, of personal response and decision, because the recognition of meaning leads to further questions which society and school cannot answer. This is how our freedom is supposed to be engaged by school.

I think we believe that our meaningless curriculum may at least have the value of leaving it up to the child or the family to create a narrative of meaning.

But looking through the schemes, going to the lessons, discussing school with pupils, it is clear that children do not experience the curriculum as an introduction to the totality of reality and therefore an introduction to their search for meaning.

Brilliant teachers often climb out of the curriculum. They instinctively expand their teaching to allow content to mean something for the pupil. Thank God for them because the search for meaning, which should be the organizational principle of every curriculum has been wholly ignored in the creation of our national one.

Chapter 5

SELF-CENSORSHIP

The Silent Treatment

The most common judgment I overhear when supervising pupils on the astro-turf is: "That is sick."

This strange phrase only entered the demotic vocabulary of Liverpool College around 2010 and had a slow start, a low R rate as we would now say. But it has become, after a period of linguistic contagion, a very common expression of approbation. Indeed, a highlight for me was when it was reported to me that a group of boys in Year 11 had described me to their parents as sick.

Sick means socially cool, morally good, aesthetically pleasing. It is a word that is synonymous to a thumb's up or yes to whatever it is describing. On the astro-turf, the opposite of "sick" is "sly", a slightly older word usually restricted to ethical commentary. This word describes morally cowardly action.

During lockdown I have been thinking about the words of approbation and reproof most commonly used by educators in our school. It has long struck me that most of us in school judge pupils and even their work in three broadly positive categories: useful, sensible, hard working.

In this respect being at school is a bit like being Thomas the Tank Engine. In the Benthamite Victorian nightmare that is the Thomas the Tank Engine series, Thomas is forever being praised for his heroic exploits on the track. The phrase, "you are a useful engine", is the highest praise that Sir Topham Hatt gives to Thomas. The young locomotive positively beams in response. His purpose is fulfilled. He is deemed useful by the owner of the railway line. Teachers love to use sensible as well. Sir

Topham Hatt, I seem to remember, uses this word a few times to describe Thomas also. To be sensible is to work productively and compliantly inside conditions which the school has set up for education and success. Particularly among younger pupils, where the socialization to community life is of utmost importance, being sensible is the great compliment. Teachers also love a hard worker. They are hard-working themselves and effort and attitude are essential to a functioning school. There are countless examples of hard-working pupils in our school. We praise their effort and hold this work ethic in high esteem.

There is one word of judgment and approbation which I rarely hear in school beyond Year 3. Beautiful. This adjective and its noun, beauty, are not part of the conversation of judgment at school. There is the cynical explanation for this, namely that like Hobbes' description of life itself, school, particularly a city secondary, is a pretty brutal and functional place. It certainly appears so when you are on the astro-turf.

But beauty has been banned from schools for some time now. It is long gone. I do not mean that the campus is not beautiful, or the poems we study are not beautiful, or that the periodic table is not beautiful, or that the art work of children hanging everywhere is not beautiful or that the actions and gestures of selfless care, charity and empathy are not beautiful. I only mean that we never talk about beauty.

During lockdown of course, we are rediscovering how much of our joy, our passion, and even our motivations are a response to beauty. Consciousness of beauty has impinged for example in our greater appreciation of the natural world.

I have learned that beauty's exile from school is one of the few things that we cannot blame on Ofsted or the government. We have been removing any discussion of this subject from education for about 100 years now. No one seems to miss it. Or at least they do not say they do. It is nevertheless interesting that we can discuss so many human experiences in school but apparently not the experience of beauty. In a sense the story of what happened to beauty is the story of the silent treatment we give so many subjects in school. It seems an innocuous little word by itself, hardly as controversial as immigration, transgender surgeries for children, abortion, Brexit, right wing terrorism, euthanasia, or voting rights for 16-year olds, all subjects we run sessions on and discuss with our pupils at length. But hidden inside this word beauty is a dangerous bomb, which could explode so many plans and systems. Once we discovered the explosive inside the word, we decided to put it away and forget about it.

If you think that perhaps this subject should properly belong to a discussion in art or music class, I have to tell you that the official approach in art education is that beauty itself is not a useful modality or paradigm for discussing art. To say that something is beautiful will not get you marks. It is deemed a meaningless observation, like saying you like something. To speculate about why it is or is not beautiful will also not score well because, of course, it cannot be scored. Even in art we describe the objective effect, not the internal experience. Ever since Kant wrestled beauty to the ground and determined in his not inconsiderable head that it was a subjective experience, is has been dropped from the discourse of what education should be about. A few centuries later and it has disappeared entirely. Even in art.

It is a feature of our curriculum that, whereas someone like Einstein spoke about the beauty of physics, mathematics and the universe itself as his reason to study it, we have silenced or censored ourselves on the topic in school. When I visit a classroom, it is not only the search for truth as represented by "the answer!", or the desire to be good, that is motivating pupils. Some are struck by the beauty of something, by its inherent attraction, but this amazement will not be discussed or explored.

This is in many ways a reduction or deliberate shrinkage of the totality of reality. So much of what I do, say, feel, buy, dislike, listen to or look at, wear, or love is triggered, motivated and driven by my conception of the beautiful, or if we must use the astro-turf term my experience of what is "sick". My response to beauty is the most unique thing about me, much more than mere taste or fashion. It is in fact one of the main ways I am moved and the way in which I relate to everything I learn and want to remember.

I stumbled across a fragment of a poem by Sappho, Fragment 16 in an article about beauty in an on-line encyclopedia of philosophy published by Stanford. This was serendipitous as Sappho is also a poet studied in the A Level Classical Civilization syllabus. Here was a possible connection between discussion of beauty and something actually studied in our school. Sappho is exactly the sort of author one would expect to find in an A level syllabus. She is an enigmatic and utterly fascinating figure and tradition records her as the first lyric poet and the first poet to write about interiority, inner feelings. She is one of the few female authors from antiquity whose work survives and her residence on the island of Lesbos and her own name are part of the etymology of the words lesbian and sapphic. The poem provides an early understanding of the connection between beauty and our deepest longing. I translate Sappho 16 as:

Some consider an army of horsemen,
others a whole fleet of ship,
still others infantry,
the most beautiful thing you can see on this dark earth,
but I say it is the one you love and desire.
It is quite easy to explain,
it is understandable for all,
The most beautiful woman in the world, Helen,
abandoned the best of men and husbands,
went off to Troy, just like that,
forgetting her daughter
and her beloved parents.
*   Aphrodite moved her.*
Anactoria is not here, and I think of her,
I prefer her swaying lovely gait,
and her radiant face,

to all the armed chariots of the Lydians
and their soldiers, and their weapons.

The poem is studied as part of a unit in the specification called Love and Relationships. Its study requires a careful analysis of poetic structure, allusions and compositional antecedents and references and exploration of Greek views of homosexuality. The examiners will have plenty of material to formulate questions. I am willing to wager my mortgage however that there are two questions that will definitely not be asked:

"Do you find this poem beautiful? What attracts you to it?"

"Do you agree with Sappho's understanding of beauty?"

When we talk or don't talk about beauty, we are talking about or ignoring attraction, longing, and judgment. Our own experience teaches us that our experience of beauty, wherever we find it, is a powerful factor in our love for our partner, our subject, our job, our house, our love for our life. But we do not mention it.

It is not possible to undertake a philosophical study of aesthetics from Plato to Scruton in school. Nor it is necessary to impose on children the sort of lesson a geography teacher colleague of mine used to inflict on pupils in which he put a symphony of Sibelius on the turntable and asked his class to close their eyes, and imagine Finland. But, it is easy to imagine that we could open up the discussion about whether something strikes our pupils or ourselves as beautiful and why in almost every part of school life. In doing so, we would be exploring and also developing an understanding of the beauty of reality in all its totality.

The reason we do not do this is fear. When we share our views of our experience of the beautiful we are talking about something very personal. We worry that we might offend, or unleash a discussion which we cannot control and which will expose one or more of our pupils or ourselves to ridicule and embarrassment. What we fear most of all is that we may talk about mystery or God or longing or our criteria of judgment. Because we believe that anything we experience as subjective is best left out of school, we create a school where reality as our pupils actually experience it is neither presented nor discussed. Beauty is a bomb. A strict rationalism and objectivity are our protection and comfort blanket, our Trumpian wall, against it, keeping the messy stuff outside even as our pupils try to make sense of one of the most powerful realities they experience without it being allowed into school.

It would take very little to make a small space in our schemes of work in any and every subject to discuss beauty, and attraction. Perhaps, ultimately, we ourselves are not persuaded enough of the beauty of reality to enthusiastically share it with our pupils. We have come to believe that introducing someone to reality is introducing them into something of neutral value and no particular beauty, a fact

not a gift.   As they would say on the astro-turf:
"That is just sly."

Chapter 6

VALUES EDUCATION

What Should I Do? Can My British Values Lesson Help Me?

The Prime Minister made a highly anticipated speech to the nation on May 10th 2020, about the plan to ease the Coronavirus induced lockdown. Millions tuned in to be released from their stay at home orders.

During a typical table thumping and gesticulating oration into the camera, he told us that the crisis would change us for the better, we would, he said, become "more sharing." I had never come across this use of the word sharing in adjectival form before. At first, I thought he might have misspoken and meant to say that we would all become more caring.

The one thing I am pretty certain about is that he did not mean to say that we would actually share more, employing the active sense of that verb with a real and substantial object attached. The cabinet would have vetoed such a bold declaration.

Here in a glimpse we perceive the problem of values education. For a while it was a rage, an unstoppable enthusiasm. All schools seemed determined to include some more values or character education in their curricula. A few education secretaries back, Nicky Morgan began to promote the excellent work of the Jubilee Centre for Character and Virtues. Schools should do more to make kids better people. In fact, we should try to teach them to be better people or at least understand what that would look like, or how one might go about thinking about becoming a better person. In the case of the Jubilee Centre this is a serious enterprise conducted with serious research by serious researchers. In the case of Boris Johnson, we have an excellent representation of the rather haphazard way we approach the problem in school.

Sharing is a great way to reflect on this because sharing is an action, a value even, which is universally praised. Visit any reception class and the child who shares is immediately awarded a high- pitched word of praise with a sticker on top. Tears in the reception playground are often because someone will not share, a reality so unfair, so contrary to an obvious moral law, that it is immediately brought to the teacher's attention. I have always been struck by the very much more highly defined sense of right and wrong of pupils in reception and their expectation of justice, that fundamental human desire. Somehow years of school do not by themselves improve this sense.

There can be no objection to Boris' suggestion that we become more sharing. It is rather like saying we should all become more lovely. What would this becoming more sharing look like? Or even sharing or caring more? Is Boris suggesting that we should share much more or maybe even everything: our houses, cars, wives, kids, pets, towels and toothbrushes? Or is he suggesting that more, just a little more, is enough, like maybe increasing my donation to the World Wildlife Fund. The question then is how much more. Can you share too much? Does he want us to share our school campus with young families seeking housing? What is the recommended level of sharing? Will he publish guidance on this?

Pupils sometimes enjoy the moralistic lectures that constitute values education. They already know the answer the teacher wants them to give, the opinion they ought to hold, and they can be certain there will be no examination. Indeed, this is the one area where the school does not seem to have all the answers, and failing to possess them, does not ask its pupils difficult questions.

Schools have literally grappled with the question of whether any teaching can make a person or even a whole country better, for thousands of years. In the very biting example of Plato's <u>Protagoras</u>, the conclusion is that it is not possible to teach a person moral excellence or character. When this conclusion is agreed, the immediate question back by one of Socrates' interlocutors is: "Well, how do we learn to be morally excellent? If it is not teachable, how is it learnable?"

In schools, we are compelled to set aside such difficulty and serve up a sort of effort to communicate and teach values and ethical standards. The government through Ofsted insists we do some values education. Our response to this compulsion is a programme of presentation of mostly politically inspired ethical themes. The aim of which is certainly uncontroversial. In fact, it could best be summed up as an invitation to pupils to become more sharing, rather than to share more.

As various topics are discussed and proposed, the kids understand, as they lean back in their chairs, that this is pure harmless propaganda from the government ethics department. It is uncontentious good stuff. "The school needs me to believe this. The government needs me to think this. Thinking this means I will not be bullied on social media or called any number of words and names. Being a good person is good. Being a bad person is not something I want to be."

The effect of watching the plays, films, presentations, lectures, and small group discussions which make up our school's attempt to teach ethics directly is a little bit like dropping in on a Manichean morality play. There are stock characters and the moral is clear. Dolphin good, fisherman bad. Elephant excellent, elephant hunter horrible. Human rights lawyer excellent, Donald Trump bad. Maybe this works up until the age of 10. But by 18 this stuff does not encourage any moral questioning because it does not reflect the complexity of moral decision making.

However, we can all rejoice that these efforts at moral correction are not all in vain. In some respects, schools have been phenomenally successful in attacking some horrible habits of pupils and staff. In my lifetime and in my career, schools were riddled with overt racism, homophobic bullying, blatant sexism and an almost pathological culture of teacher-ignored teasing and humiliation of anything that was remotely different from anything or anyone else. These behaviours in my experience were the norm, not the exception. Together with the rest of society, we have created a zero tolerance for ancient evils in schools. Everyday there is ample evidence the battle is not yet won, but the fight has been effectively joined.

A typical example of a values education presentation at our school might be a visit from people who are leading a campaign to remove plastic straws from the seas. Their cause is incontrovertibly a good one. Indeed, there are very many good causes which come to our campus every year, explaining, usually effectively and sympathetically, some problem in the world and how we can do something about it either by raising our awareness or by raising money. Preferably both. Ethics here becomes reduced to the support of various charities, however noble.

Within this context of unambiguous value education, pupils are especially cynical about the term British values. As they grow older they realize that what is being presented is neither British not really a value. The complexity, for example, of the case of a person who sells all their earthly possessions to support the widows and children of Isis fighters in Iraq is not dealt with. The great trouble about free speech, an issue which actually effects many pupils because the exercise of the freedom of speech on line has big impacts in their social and emotional lives, is also simplified to a digestible bowl of popcorn.

The result of this programme is an enormous amount of partisan political engagement and activism and lots of charitable enterprise. As the years roll by, school mock elections are becoming ever more hotly contested. Indeed, the shallow and spiteful nature of political dialogue in the country is reflected in the school setting, despite the best efforts of teachers. The ethical world has shrunk to a number of causes and, frankly, a lot of sentimentality about those causes and the good one can do by aligning oneself to them. It is difficult to argue against political engagement, charitable giving and activism, particularly since so many people worry about the supposed selfishness of the young.

A serious attempt at values education would not seek to establish what is good or bad in such simplistic and overtly political terms. Our starting point should surely be the sovereignty of the conscience of an individual person and how one can develop one's conscience. This would, if we were serious, include careful examination of real-world cases, initially with no clear political lobbies. Tough situations faced by doctors or by teachers, by parents, by lovers, by business owners, and by children would be presented and explored in their complexity. We would work hard to give pupils the confidence to reason morally from principles, able to identify the values which are at stake, and where they clash which ones they think should have priority. We might stress ethical dilemmas rather than political projects within our curriculum. We might ask regularly in examinations how a particular dilemma or ethical problem facing a person, country, institution or even the world, relates to other dilemmas. We might consider that the quality of the moral reasoning in the answer should be part of the mark scheme, in the way that we have been able to introduce percentage marking for spelling and grammar.

Our great stress could be on notions of honour and conscience, both of which, like beauty, have beaten a long retreat from school, and for similar reasons. From pupils thus introduced to an examination of the ethical dimension of life would emerge a genuinely fresh political and social view rather than a conscripted army for the lobbies of various causes.

We could challenge ourselves to develop not a curriculum of the study and examination of the virtues as philosophical categories or an introduction to all sorts of charities in the world but a gradual introduction to the way ethics impinge on every life and how people have come to their ethical conclusions. We could be determined to give our pupils confidence that they have a clearly developed conscience to rely on when such dilemmas arise and a method of discussing their ethical concerns. We aim for all these things in numeracy and literacy skills. I do not see why we could not do this in the case of values education.

This is what we would do if we wanted pupils to share more rather than to become "more sharing".

Chapter 7

CAREERS
EDUCATION

Working on the World

Motivating teachers and motivating pupils are two very different things. The social and moral purpose of our school, its role in society, can be clearly defined for teachers. In my experience, teachers understand immediately what I mean when I say that the moral purpose of the school in our context is to ensure that every child, regardless of background or disadvantage, can exercise the moral right to a good education.

In chapter 1, I explained how much harder it can be to define exactly what we mean when we use the word education. It is far easier to say that our school is about justice, about fairness, about making sure that everyone has an equal opportunity to develop all their potential. Indeed, the most common definition I use of our school is that it is an instrument for the destruction of the effects of disadvantage. In my experience, teachers are motivated by these considerations. If they are not, they usually leave teaching rather quickly. School as a driver of social justice is a motivational definition which works for teachers.

We are not the only school with a defined moral purpose. Such definitions of the purposes of school are ubiquitous. They absolutely infuse the entire educational landscape. As a society we are deeply conscious of a social wound, namely that where you are born and to whom you are born and even where you live is a more powerful determinant of the course of your life than any other characteristic or fact about you.

This clear moral purpose is seldom shared with the pupils as individuals. We do not like to reveal to a child that our moral purpose is to drag them out of a category of disadvantage. And even if we do reveal it, the effect is unsurprisingly not at all motivational. During lockdown for example, it has been difficult to persuade the vulnerable and disadvantaged to come to school. This is in part because they do not want to be labelled in any way. The social and moral purpose of school and the motivation for participation in school is therefore less clear to pupils than it is to teachers.

With pupils we use phrases like "making the most of your talents", or "getting ready for a great job" to try to explain the purpose of school to pupils. I do not think I am mistaken when I perceive that eyes glaze over slightly when these attempts at motivations are deployed. They are too vague.

Our school has a wonderful Latin motto and, after a concerted effort, almost all pupils know what it means and therefore know that they are going to a school based upon the motto "not only the intellect, but also character." But again, worthwhile as this motto is in explaining the general philosophy which underpins the curriculum and the purposes of the school, it can hardly be described as an effective motivator on its own.

Some might argue that a school does not need to worry about providing a clear social and moral purpose or motivator for its activity to pupils. But I am afraid that this does not comport with our own experience as adults and teachers. There are plenty of times when we cry out to high heaven "why, oh why" and then we must remind ourselves of some clear social or moral purpose to get going again in our life and our job. Why do we not think pupils need similarly clear and cogent motivation? A teacher gets paid. A pupil does not. The motivation to go to school is not as great as might generally be supposed. In Liverpool more than 12% of secondary pupils miss more than one day per fortnight during any academic year. That number is even greater in sixth forms. In seeking to motivate the persistently absent, I have resorted pathetically to the educational equivalent of the parental exasperation, "because I said so," by telling parents and pupils they must come to school "because it is the law."

In truth, schools are terrible at motivational branding. Nike's "Just Do it" makes me want to buy a pair of trainers and run down to the park. There is no attempt to brand ourselves in motivational terms, to make it comprehensibly cool to go to school.

Part of the problem of course is the fences that surround British schools. It is easier to escape from what was formerly Alcatraz than to get out of a school. There are of course good reasons for this. But from a branding, marketing and image perspective children experience school as a place behind a fence from a young age. Fences are not exciting.

Recently, educator friends from Denmark visited us. They were especially struck by our high and impenetrable fences and gates, of which we are justifiably proud. I had visited their school which is a boarding school for children facing severe emotional difficulties and discovered they had not one fence on their large campus. I tried to explain our concerns about intruders, children absconding, controlling any possible lockdown, delineating the authority of the school in clear geographical terms. But when I had finished my defensive apologia, I realized that our motivational branding starts off with a fence. Fortunately, there are some things in school and about school which in my experience always motivate pupils.

I have observed that the recent emphasis on careers education is always accompanied by pupil motivation. Careers activities such as personal interest and aptitude profiles, psychological and psychometric testing, individual interviews, career fairs and days usually get a very enthusiastic response.

It seems there is in fact a sweet spot where the narcissism of teenagers meets quite happily with the economy-above-all approach of ministers. Because that is what is driving the government emphasis on careers education. There is concern that British children's interest and study choices do not coincide with the demands of the labour market. Careers education, and also the aggressive promotion of apprenticeships and technical education, as well as the glamorization of STEM subjects, are a response to this problem. The amazingly titled national Gatsby Benchmarks for careers education reveal this quite clearly. The best schools will have a careers programme which includes and consist of:

- A settled and established careers programme
- Learning from career and labour market information.
- Addressing the needs of each pupil.
- Linking curriculum learning to careers.
- Encounters with employers and employees.
- Experiences of workplaces.

- Encounters with further and higher education.
- Personal guidance.

Every school in the country is being systematically encouraged and instructed to pursue these benchmarks. Here we see the school being ordered to emphasize its role in creating *homo-economicus*, the future workforce.

The reason why pupils like careers education more than most other things in school is because the process of careers education allows them to place themselves, their "I", in a future away from school. Apparently, they experience that future away from school as an attractive place for them to be.

It is revealing that we use the word career for this rather than job. A career has the idea of a journey in it. It stretches out beyond the concept of having or getting a job. Careers education is therefore inherently more open in its possibilities than jobs education.

Career assumes a narrative, and I think, this appeals to pupils. "The story of my life" is, unless you have been infused with total nihilism, still an attractive and motivational theme when you are young. It smacks of what St Thomas Aquinas would term pure "*potentia*", the power of pure potential open- ended possibility.

I have occasionally observed a similar enthusiasm in pupils for projects. Almost any community or charity project led by or driven by pupils in the school, particularly one they thought of themselves, tends to create motivation for school. When pupils themselves say they want to start an eco-committee and sort our recycling in the school, levels of enthusiasm and motivation can reach very high, and from a headteacher's point of view, impressive levels.

These enthusiastic responses reveal a pupil appetite to engage with, experience, and dream about what they could do in the world if they were no longer constrained by their youth and by their school. My own experience comports with this sentiment. I spent a lot of time in school from a very early age dreaming about what I might do or become. These Walter Mitty-like ruminations placed me in all sorts of contests and situations, very far beyond the mere notion of career. When dreaming of my future I dreamt of course about a partner in life, some noble service to mankind, a house, freedom, fame. I tried to picture myself in various heroic and morally sound situations. I was particularly attracted to situations where my love of action and leadership could come to fruition.

Sadly, because of the metaphorical fence between our school and the world, many children I meet today do not have such fantasies. It's possible that their parents do not have an expectation or habit of discussing future plans and hopes with their children. It is also possible that school has eliminated these reveries with a constrained and narrow understanding of the human desire to work on the world in all its facets and factors and replaced this desire with the concept of a career.

From simple observation of the play in a reception class, one can observe the motivational effect of the opportunity to work on the world, to engage with reality and create something in it. The total motivation and concentration of a group of 4 -year olds as they set about playing in an imaginary fort reveals a deep truth about how schools could motivate pupils. On display here is one of the deepest desires we all have, the vocation of every human being, an inescapable urge. We want to "do" something, to make something in the world, to create a new structure, a new culture, a new experience, a new family, a new idea. We want to be creative and have a unique and real impact on reality, not only for ourselves but also for others.

If we are really honest, school is frequently experienced by pupils as an exercise in delayed gratification of this desire. Our proposal to pupils from the day they leave reception is that now is the time for them to get the knowledge and the skills so that one day at some point in the future they will be able to "do" something.

This is the source of pupil enthusiasm for careers day. Pupils see the end at the light of the tunnel. They understand the imminent fulfilment of what we promised them since they were about 5 years old. If you do this and this and this, you will have a chance to pursue your dreams later. Now, as they explicitly engage with careers education, that day is finally at hand.

From the school's point of view, the enforced delay to the development of the pupil's natural instinct to "do" something in the world, an instinct which school have controlled, subdued and curbed, is called to an immediate and sudden self-resuscitation. Schools now want to use this light at the end of the tunnel to motivate pupils to work harder in their revision for their examinations and to aim higher. This technique of so -called aspiration is in fact what the narrator of <u>The Great Gatsby</u>, not the

Gatsby benchmarks, describes as the nightmare of the tension between Gatsby the individual and America and its ideal.

 "So we beat on, boats against the current, borne back ceaselessly into the past."

The experience of watching pupils embrace action in their own community, particularly action directed by themselves, should teach us to approach schools and also careers education differently. Rather than making links between what I am learning in my reading of <u>The Great Gatsby</u> and any possible career as a plumber or garage mechanic, or self-made and deluded millionaire, like the government is suggesting, we should open the school itself up as a place for active work by pupils. I have never understood our fear about letting kids wash dishes, including for money, in the dining room, or paint the walls of their form room, or build a new garden bed, build computer programmes, start charities. The idea that the best preparation for working on the world is to not work on it at all is manifestly crazy. We seem terrified to make the school a place where the instincts of the building of a fantasy fort in reception can be refined until these same pupils are founding an eco- committee, producing plays, selling an app. The drive to work on the world must be educated and channeled. It cannot be developed through an artificial postponement and separation from the world in a managerially controlled zero-risk safety zone called school. For some pupils, the enthusiasm to work on the world does not ever return after its school-induced hibernation.

Working on the world also expands our conception of a career far beyond a simple equivalence with paid work. Are we really suggesting that a young man who decides to stay at home to raise his children is a person who has no career? Are the efforts of the army of volunteers and club, church and society members, of parents, friends, gardeners, allotment owners, and kite flyer club chairmen who make up a properly democratic society not examples of some serious work on the world?

Is our proposal to young people really that their relationship with reality in the future is going to consist of leisure, paid work, and consumption only, in a cycle of everlasting tedium and passivity.

"Working on the World" is a slogan that pupils could understand. It could answer once and for all the sharpest pupil question: "What is school for?" If a child asked why she should come to school, we would be able to say because we need her to help us work on the school so that she learns to work on the world. It would make clear to a pupil in every year group in school that they are serving a very active apprenticeship in active engagement in society at every level of human activity, in our culture, in the environment, in the arts, in their community. There would still need to be a fence. But this time it would be needed to keep the energy, motivation, enthusiasm and engagement inside school from spilling out into the waiting world rather than being needed to keep the bustling world with all its possibility locked out.

Chapter 8

PASTORAL CARE

The Tears of Things and the Tears of School

Our school contains within a small community the gamut of human emotion, experience, and drama. That is what makes our school a compelling place to work and fruitful place to develop as a human being. I am not only referring to the development of pupils toward full maturity. I am also describing the way working at school deepens the maturity or exposes the immaturity of adults and forces everyone to come face to face with a daily barrage of human brokenness.

Amongst the joys, the laughter, the successes, the relationships, the fun and the activities in every second of school life, is the unspeakable sadness of human life. In fact, my own memory is that I began an awareness of this when I was at school while reading Virgil's <u>Aeneid</u> Book I with the Latin teacher I adored. Virgil uses the phrase "lacrimae rerum", "the tears of things", when describing Aeneas looking at a mural depicting the Trojan war. In this moment of looking, he is able to remember the bitter experience of the war over his old city and home, the loss of his wife, father and friends, and his exile and wanderings. My teacher explained that the phrase was ambiguous grammatically and difficult to translate but it had always had a clear meaning for him, namely that the burdens of sorrow and suffering were the essential experience of being a person. I told him that I felt somehow that he must be right, that the beauty and meaning of the phrase did resonate with me, but that I had not experienced such sorrow and tears in things. He smiled rather ruefully at this. Since then, I have looked on the world differently.

We attend funerals of children, colleagues and parents, snatched out of families through accidents, sudden cardiac arrests, slowly wasting diseases, or even more gruesome circumstance. We are the recipients of disclosures and accounts of abuse, neglect, self-harm, suicide attempts, drug abuse, overdoses, and shocking betrayal and cruelty. We engage with young people so angry at the world, at themselves, at us that they are not able to speak but only hiss in rage.

Kids confess or at least share their fears with us. Fears of crime, fears of uncertainty about sexual identity and acceptance of that identity, fears about sleeping, fears about waking, fears about their neighbourhood, fears about their Instagram account, fears even about their fears. They share with us their experience of brutal home lives, often exacerbated by family breakdown, sometimes repeated, by new partners and parents in the home. They are often not able to find the words of their frustration because of an injustice, a slight.

Their number is comparatively small but the pathology afflicting them is usually a deep one. They are restless within the psychological boundary of school. They disturb other people, break the good order of school life, harass their peers and their teachers. They are at war with the school, coming from some place of alienation and anger through the gates every morning.

From the desk of the headteacher, these intense expressions of anger, pain and suffering can and sometimes do completely drown any other experience of school. I forget about all the children who are not experiencing these things this way. I can only remember the suffering of a child or a family. Theirs are silent screams that bounce around the walls of the school, heard by the staff who cannot forget them. They are the tears of things.

The term pastoral care is used to describe the response of the school to this reality. There are so many acts of pastoral care in any given day that if you had to take an inventory of them, everyone working in a school from the receptionist and dinner ladies to the headteacher would be filling pages of lists and notes every day. There is a constant flow of response to the need perceived in, or expressed by, pupils. But even that sometimes does not seem enough.

It is interesting to consider what model shapes our response. I think one model is the school as hospital. I know any parent reading this reflection will find this an amazing confession: a hospital? But in truth, many people at Liverpool College do work by necessity in a paradigm of the school as a hospital. Here the emotionally wounded, the pained, the neglected, the confused, and the undiagnosed are treated and cared for. Here a first diagnosis of the problem which is causing pain or poor behaviour or poor progress or low self-esteem or anxiety or depression is made, so that further investigations and studies can reveal the deeper and more comprehensive picture of the pathology.

Another model is the school as prison. Pupils never tire of pointing out to me that principal's detention Friday after school and internal exclusion feel a little like what prison must feel like. They are asked to sit quietly in a room, able to do their work or read a book, but not play on a phone. They are in fact deprived of their freedom of movement and free time to teach them that their behaviour cannot be tolerated and must improve.

Another model of school is school as community or family. This is the model that schools are perhaps not consciously pursuing but certainly the model which most frequently accords with our school's perception of itself. But, as one fellow headteacher told me, families and communities are for most places of safety and acceptance and for others places of alienation, violence and pain.

The dominant model of school, is actually the model of the state, the social contract. Our school may present itself or conceive of itself in a variety of ways, but ultimately, it is a public body, governed by laws, regulated by law. The school's actions are reviewable in law. The pupils and their parents have an enormous long list of rights in regard to their dealings with school which are enshrined and enforceable by law. The school has rights also which are enforceable by law, including the right to decide to remove a pupil permanently from the community.

None of the models help a child who is suffering. That is because none of the models is able to grasp fully the dimensions of suffering as a human condition. Suffering is not equivalent to pain or hurt or frustration. Suffering is not fundamentally caused or relieved by good or bad hospitalization. Our wonderful staff can attest to innumerable instances where we have helped a pupil and their family in every possible way but have not been able to help their suffering.

Suffering arises from an experience of why, why me, why us, why this, why now. It arises out of experiences that seem unjust, unforeseen, and inexplicable to oneself. Schools are very bad at distinguishing between pain and suffering. Our preference, as professionals is to keep things at the level of dealing with what are called "the issues" rather than the existential experience of the suffering.

For example, when a child loses a parent we might attend the funeral, organize a conversation about grief counselling, set up a regular contact for the parent and the child. Here grief and suffering are things to be managed, to be overcome, to return the situation as fast as possible to the situation before the suffering began. An impossible quest. Of course, it makes sense to do all we can to relieve physical, emotional and psychological pain and suffering as soon as possible but what I have noticed is that the things which actually achieve this relief are not the things "best practice" tells us to do.

What seems to have some positive effect are those unforeseen, unplanned and "unprofessional" situations where we take the risk of stepping out of the hospital, prison or social contract model and enter a model of companionship. We are no longer "the school" with its authority and power and knowledge and recourse to policies, plans, EHATs, EHCPs, MASHs and all the other acronyms of the bureaucratization of suffering. We are simply there. Something stirs inside us and we manage to prioritize the urge in our hearts to simply respond by saying: "I know you are suffering, I do not know why you have to suffer, but I am here for you, and I am going to be here with you to suffer with you." Such a sentence has never been uttered on most school campuses but the actions and attitudes to which the sentence point are occasionally found. In those situations, something new happens and the suffering of a person or family is not solved, which suffering never can be, but is shared.

This much more closely, of course, resembles the model of a healthy family than any other model.

I do for this reason always regret the prevalent use of exclusion, particularly permanent exclusion also known as expulsion, in schools generally and in our school. There are of course moments when a person cannot stay on the campus of the school because it would be intolerable to her or his victim and would send totally the wrong message. But the use of permanent exclusion in our schools sends exactly the wrong message to the wrong people and it prevents us from offering the companionship that the victim as well as the perpetrator need. It is the ultimate act of rejection and state sanctioned isolation. I have increasingly regretted permanent exclusion and tried to find solutions that keep the companionship with a pupil and his or her family going despite a pupil not being able to remain on campus. These efforts are not always appreciated because some believe that this companionship may undermine the good order and social contract that underpins school.

About 84,000 adults are in prison in the UK at any given time. Tens of thousands of pupils are in alternative provision, or have been excluded permanently from a school at any given time. If we are serious about any model other than the prison or the social contract model, then these statistics should pierce our souls. This really is the face of failure to be imaginative about the ways we can continue to accompany someone who must leave our campus, or who is not able to cope with our school.

I have a colleague who led a school where a pupil died in a car crash during holiday time because the driver of the car who was also a pupil was drunk. The driver survived the crash and was sentenced to prison. My colleague, despite what I assume was considerable pressures inside the school community, did not exclude the pupil permanently and the school visited the pupil in prison. That is the model of school as the community of the broken, a model of companionship which resonates with our vision of ourselves as educators.

Our schools do not do well for people who suffer because we never talk about suffering. We have in short no educational philosophy of suffering. Where in school does a child learn what suffering is? Where is it explained that to live a full life is to experience suffering yourself and to experience the suffering of others? Where do we allow pupils to discover there are no solutions to suffering except companionship? The topic is not easy and therefore partial and reduced views of suffering and its supposed "cure" are advanced. These vary from restorative justice models to all sorts of other techniques which are little better than quackery when it comes to the child who is truly suffering.

We name every possible behaviour and every possible problem, but the fundamental human experience of suffering is reduced in school by our unwillingness to recognize its mysterious quality. Here is something no one understands, no one can solve, for which no pill, no course of counselling, no solution as such can be found, only the mystery of the human capacity to share suffering. Our professionalism and our view of ourselves as an educational hospital make us in fact a broken community, where there are strict limits and boundaries placed on our companionship with the broken. We reach for the social contract model when the hospital model fails, by-passing notions of true community, or family. The result is not only isolation and further suffering for our pupils and their families but also a reduction in us as educators, a repression of human sympathy and empathy which stunts us and reduces us.

These are the tears of things, so visible in school. The tears will always flow, but our response can flow from broken community to community for the broken.

Chapter 9

PUPIL VOICE

Freedom and the Hypothesis of School

I had heard about "deep dives" before the inspectors undertook one in our school. The deep dive is unrelated to scuba or submarines. It is a hilarious term for a very unfunny thing: the rigorous inspection of the educational processes of a particular part of a school. For example, inspectors might go into an English department for a day and turn over the educational furniture for a few hours, visit lessons, study the work of pupils, inspect whether the curriculum is sufficiently challenging and actually being implemented. The deep dive includes interviews with the subject leaders, teachers and pupils. Deep dive is a bit of a euphemism. Ransack is a word that might more accurately be employed.

I was amazed to learn that these so-called deep dives, for all their comprehensiveness, were not the end of the matter. I had assumed that the deep dive would come to some sort of conclusion. But it turned out that the deep dive led instead to a thing referred to as the "hypothesis". The hypothesis was the idea that the inspectors would then go and try to verify. So, for example, they might conclude a deep dive in computer studies and have discovered that homework was not regularly set in that department. This would then lead to a hypothesis that would be : "This school does not set homework." The hypothesis would then be inspected the next day and either proven or not proven. Inspection became a process of the verification of the hypothesis derived from the deep dive.

Thankfully, everyone who works at our school knows more about the way inspectors work then I do, so my incredulity and dismay at this idea of hypotheses being tested throughout the school was not shared. My colleagues knew that there would be such things as hypotheses which were going to be tested. They threw the word around with acuity and skill. Hypothesis this, hypothesis that.

When the inspectors left and the war was all over, I began to think about this concept of hypothesis. What interested me was not the value of the concept of hypothesis in any evaluation of the school by me, or a teacher, or a parent, or an outside body. I wondered instead how a pupil could develop, or at least be helped to develop, a hypothesis about the school which could serve as a criterion of judgment on it.

In short, what would the hypothesis be if we were going to find a hypothesis a pupil could use to determine whether a school is working for her. This hypothesis would be radically different from the hypothesis derived at by studying schemes of work, curricula, grade books, assessments and all the stuff inspectors look at. We could never share such data with a pupil in Year 4. It would be totally meaningless. Secondly, it would not lead to a useful hypothesis for that pupil.

The hypothesis for the effectiveness of aspirin that a pupil could use would be that upon taking the aspirin she experiences that she feels a little better. If she feels materially worse she would conclude that the aspirin is not working for her.

What would the equivalent be for a pupil in a school?

It is not yet clear to me why such a hypothesis has never been attempted. One reason may be that a school is a very supplier focused organization. The last thing we want to do is give our customers a criterion for judging us. We talk endlessly of provision and educational settings without ever consulting the possible customer or client. This makes some sense, because most people know what they like to eat but do not know what their child should learn in school. They trust us to get it right for their children. This trust means we do not have to give them a criterion for judging us or a hypothesis against which we should be tested. But what is the criterion we have given or taught our pupils so that they themselves can determine the effectiveness of a school?

It may be helpful to think of a nationalized railroad when thinking about an education system. Many people would argue that a train that gets you safely and in comfort to your destination on time is in fact the best possible train. The criterion of judgment would therefore relate to the destination. This is in fact the way we want pupils to think about school.

When I was a teenager, I told my headmaster in the US during a rare meeting in his office that the school council survey showed conclusively that we as pupils thought that our education should be more open to the real world and include more dances with girls schools. After he jocularly pointed out to me that inviting girls from Maryland to our school in Washington DC was equivalent to transporting females across state lines for entertainment purposes and should therefore perhaps be deemed a felony, he made a more general and serious point of objection. He said that he felt certain that it would only be much later in our lives that we would understand or appreciate the education we had received and that the proper people to survey about the value of the education the school provided were alumni over the age of 25.

My headmaster took seriously what most headteachers, pupils, teachers and parents take seriously. School needs to get us to a destination in life, to a maturity. It is from this place that we can finally understand what it was all about. The hypothesis of evaluating the effectiveness of school we want our pupils to use is one which they can only apply long after they have left school. We are saying to pupils: "When you have achieved your SATS/GCSEs A-levels/Degree/job interview/professional qualification and you have embarked upon your Happy Life, you should establish whether the school was a help or a hindrance."

There's some wisdom in this approach, because it may perhaps be foolhardy to invite a 7 year- old to reflect too deeply on whether or not the school is failing her. However, this "wait until you are older" view fails to engage the pupil in any reflection on what the effect of the experience of school is on them.

It may be helpful, if possible, to equip our pupils with a criterion of judgment on all their school activity, a hypothesis about its purposes and intentions which they can apply concurrently with those activities.

My offer for the hypothesis a pupil might use while still in school is that everything at school should make him more free. I would invite pupils to ask themselves at every instance and point of their time in school whether what they are doing and learning in school is making them more free. Currently, we only ask students whether they like something in school or whether they are learning something in school.

The hypothesis would suggest that everything you do and learn at school should enable you to free yourself from some ignorance or partial conception or mistaken view of the world, of yourself, or of other people. It should free you from prejudice and from the undue influence of the opinion of others, to free yourself from any influence other than what you have learned and experienced as the truth and the right thing to do. Freedom is the process by which we learn to engage all of reality with our best possible selves. It is what we experience when our fundamental desires for our engagement with reality are satisfied because they are rooted in our experience of what is true. When you are free you do what you know is the right thing to do, what your best self wants to do.

This understanding of freedom is not one which is commonly discussed in schools. Freedom is viewed primarily as a political condition, as I have pointed out in an earlier chapter. In our customary view, freedom exists primarily in relationship to power, the power of authority over us. That concept of freedom in school is based on a model of rights. If you asked any current Year 8 what freedom in school would look like you would get a description of anarchic licence and Lucazade-fuelled leisure, a removal, in total, of any adult authority in school.

It would not be too difficult to move beyond this rather simplistic understanding of freedom however. Pupils, I think, understand, that there is such a thing as freedom from ignorance, prejudice, peer pressure, consumerist pressures and all the things which prevent us from being who we really want to be. They understand the concept of an intellectual and psychological and emotional freedom which also accepts there has to be some order in the school for freedom itself to be achieved. In fact, I think it is a small step for most of our pupils to understand that the happier, more satisfied, more fulfilled and more purposeful a person becomes the freer they are and vice-versa.

At this point the eyes of teachers and parents glaze over. This is one provocation too far within the pages of one book. They perceive that here lies a route to chaos, disobedience and disorder. If we are going to test the hypothesis of school as a place for increasing freedom, where will it stop? Will pupils begin to refuse to do homework, refuse to go to bed on time, refuse to queue in an orderly fashion? Will we see rebellion, mutiny and revolution in the hallways of the College?

No. Our own understanding of the relationship between education and its goal of empowering freedom has been so distorted that we associate true freedom with disorder. When we think of school, the last thing that pops into our minds is the word freedom. We do acknowledge that our children develop in school. We use phrases like: "She has grown in confidence", or "Mohammed is really growing up into a fine scholar and young man", or "I can't believe how much she loves Spanish. I do not know where she gets it from." All three sentiments describe or at least acknowledge the growth and development of true freedom in a person.

In teaching pupils to apply the hypothesis that school should be helping them to become freer, they are not being invited to detach themselves in a revolutionary impulse from the work or programmes of the school. They are being invited to consider whether or not it is in fact making them more free. They are simply being given a criterion to judge what we do. A criterion which can be refined over the course of one's life and one' education. Freedom to do the right thing. Freedom to pursue the truth. Freedom to be and become who I am really meant to be and who, in my best moments, I want to be.

It is possible to suggest that this conception of growth in freedom is just another kind of learning. That the hypothesis proposed as the criterion of judgment is a semantic sleight of hand. That the concept of freedom here advanced is simply another way for a child to say: "I have learned how to this, or how to that, or what this is". The problem with the idea that the hypothesis should be "did you learn something" is precisely that if you learn something which has no impact on your life now, you will forget it. Our hearts and minds are such that we dispose of all knowledge and experience which we cannot use or which we find meaningless, repulsive or boring. It is possible to conceive of a school where children learn all sorts of things but are utterly miserable, prejudiced, and even dull.

When Jimmy says that detention is wrong because it is taking away his freedom, we could explain to him that he is not yet free because he does not want to interrupt his chemistry teacher 10 times in a lesson but he keeps doing so. When pupils, having been encouraged to test the hypothesis, complain that the diminishment of choice in puddings in the dining room is an infringement of their inalienable right to sugar and to infinite choice in pursuit of donuts, we could explain that our purpose is only to educate them to choose their nourishment so as to maximize their feeling of wellbeing, control over appetite, and purpose in their diet. In short, to lessen their enslavement to bad food and make them free to choose what to eat. They might vehemently disagree, but they would have a hypothesis they could test.

The constant discussion of the hypothesis could lead to a deeper understanding of what freedom is and especially what a free person feels and acts like. In fact, it would soon become possible to ask a pupil at the end of a lesson or other school activity how that lesson or activity has made them more free or how it has inhibited the development of their freedom.

I look forward to the day when the deep dives become deep dives about pupils explaining their growth in freedom and when pupils are able to criticise us for our true failures. Failure to help make them free.

Chapter 10

PURPOSE

Running From The Good Life

During lockdown, I have frequently recalled philosophy tutorials I attended more than 30 years ago during my university days. I had assumed when I signed up for a specific module, then called paper, that there would be a few students taking the course with me but they did not materialize. I ended up a solitary and somewhat reluctant student climbing up to a sort of garret office at the top of a grey building overlooking a Scottish beach. Here every Monday afternoon I cautiously entered my tutor's study and sat there in a state of confusion as he peppered me with questions. There was no escape. He was a very unorthodox teacher, known in the university as an enthusiastic amateur violinist who wore two hearing aids and "cranked them up" while playing in the town orchestra.

He assigned whole books of philosophy to read and said he would think of some questions when I had finished them. During one of the earliest tutorials he asked me what I would instruct him to do if he wanted to become happy. Years of Catholic school immediately kicked in as I launched a rather mystical and metaphysical and overtly Christian answer to his question. He listened, paused, and said: "No, I think I will be happier if I just go surfing."

It took a long time for me to persuade him that a life of surfing only would never make him entirely happy. At the very least he would need some friends, some food, and some other basic things. I even managed to make a small dent in his indifference with an argument that he should stop smoking his pipe. He had rejected this idea early on in our sessions when I raised the matter with him and issued a challenge back to me to the effect that if I could explain to him why living longer was desirable, he might consider no longer lighting up and billowing strongly aromatic smoke throughout the room.

This process taught me an important lesson and brought to life a key Aristotelian observation about the good life. It consists of many things, not one thing. Aristotle clearly based his model of the good life on that of a Greek, free, male and thought carefully about all the virtues such a life contained and all the various activities which would make up this life.

This enterprise of reflecting systematically on and discussing openly all the ingredients of a good life has certainly been set aside in school. There's a good reason for this. Any suggestion of anyone telling anyone else that some ways of living life are better than others is complete anathema in school.

This itself is an extraordinary situation from a historical perspective. School has always been the instrument by means of which societies pass on from one generation to another what they know, what they believe, and even what they hope for in life. This tradition most commonly included exemplars of good living, and a hierarchy of values and behaviours, some to be condemned others to be celebrated. The founders of Liverpool College, for example, were almost ridiculously certain of the content of their communication about what was good in life and what was a good life. They believed strongly that the school should propose to its pupils a Christian understanding of the meaning of life and a national or English bourgeois version of how this should be lived. They seem to have embraced this mission with what we today would view as intolerant certainty and exclusivity.

But a school today presents no such certain proposal of the good life to its pupils. Indeed, we refuse to value any activity as preferable to any other with the exception of criminal acts. The one activity which we do affirm as essential and therefore non-negotiable is what philosophers like Jurgen Habermas call discursive or deliberative democracy. In short, and it's difficult to express this thought briefly, discursive democracy is the activity where decision makers have an authentic discourse of equals, based on the radical equality of all, coming to a view which all accept as reasonable, which in turn becomes the basis of ethics and law.

This value or virtue of discursive democracy is the only one which we uphold as an absolute in school. It is entirely understandable that we uphold it in this way. Our aim is to ensure that our school produces people who are able to function in a pluralistic society where competing claims are resolved through democratic processes with respect for every single person.

To make sure this one absolute value is revered and able to dominate any other we rely heavily on policies, activities and messages in school which we believe will promote tolerance and encourage democratic participation. Usually, the values we promote or encourage are those which have in some way been codified in law. For example, we would never say to a child of consenting age that they should not have sex, (as long as they do it safely and legally) or that watching pornography degrades men and women or that people who are married should stay married, or that serving others is better than taking from them, or even that they exist to serve others rather than that other people exist to serve them. All these statements would be intolerable expressions to our pupils and parents of a personal opinion or value and one which had not been subjected to discursive democracy and enshrined in the consensus that is law.

The net effect of the school's assertion of this one supreme activity has some obvious manifestations.

The first is that pupils experience the limitations of a value system based on consensus. There's definite consensus in the world that fighting is a bad thing but there is much less of a consensus about when it is acceptable to engage in a fight. When someone bullies endlessly, or even pushes you or physically provokes you, can you retaliate? Is it possible to have any consensus or policy about this or will the matter have to be investigated and judged according to the principles of "law"? Is the value of my action ultimately determined by the standard of law? Never fight is not a realistic directive to a 13 year -old boy. Discursive democracy and its product, the law, or policy, does not cover every eventuality and the 150+ policies that cover our school are not able to be applied to every single situation and all its nuances

Secondly, the supreme value we attach to our discursive democracy model cannot by definition promote one view of the good life over any other. As a pedagogical principle, it is a negative concept, a formulation of what is not possible. The elevation of a discursive democracy model essentially says to pupils that they will have to figure out what a good life looks like themselves through experience or discuss it somewhere else because as a school we are not agreed on what a good life looks like. It is impossible for us to create a hierarchy of value or meaning and impossible to promote any vision of the truly excellent or exceptional life because we can only promote that about which there is total consensus. By its very nature, total consensus is a compromised standard which precludes the exceptional, the unusual, the transformative, the new, the extraordinary, the excellent.

Thirdly, this one supreme value of discursive democracy is, paradoxically, a value so absolute that its rejection by a pupil is not acceptable or accepted. This is a given. No discussion about it is ever undertaken or permitted. It is a value whose absolute elevation occurs without discussion. As such, discursive democracy, as experienced by a pupil in a school refers to activity undertaken by the adults in society. To a pupil, it is neither discursive nor democratic and it is an activity in which she cannot fully engage, an ideal for which there is only limited room for practice in school.

The result is a school where pupils are not asked to verify through experience, action and study a coherent proposal of true human excellence. To read about the idealism of the great educators throughout the ages, is to lament the total elimination of a true ideal of human life in our school today. When I read our pupil profile I think of how little of the truly ideal is incorporated in it. In faith schools like ours, there is, I suppose, the theoretical or legal possibility of a school proposing to its pupils that the good life is to be more like Jesus, or Moses, or Mohammed. But even in these schools like ours, in my experience, there is a lack of enthusiasm for setting out a clear proposal about what a good life looks like which can be accepted or rejected by pupils. Instead, the faith proposal enters the discursive democracy model, becomes an acceptable consensus and fails to have impact educationally as a vision of the truly excellent life.

A school which accepts the consensus of society on everything is unable to offer a vision of moral excellence and to propose to pupils that excellence as a goal. It turns out, in schools at any rate, that the elevation of discursive democracy kills off the elevation of any other virtue. The results of this in terms of pedagogy and pupil experience of school are not difficult to anticipate.

Whereas the experience of being young cries out for an engagement with ideals and for an opportunity to engage with a tradition which at least proposes a vision of human excellence, most pupils are fed a version of what the school considers a great learner looks like, not what a great person looks like.

Imagine a simple proposal to pupils. The good life consists of serving others and improving the world. This may seem a simple proposal, even if we could all agree on it (which we could not), but its adoption by a school would transform every aspect of its culture, curriculum, policy and programme. It would provide a prism and focus of tremendous intensity in the activity of the school.

If we could agree to any proposal, we could actually put it to pupils and allow them to verify from their own experience and learning whether the school is correct or not. The proposal would in fact encourage discursive democracy in school whilst also leaving room for the eccentric, the unusual, the unconventional, the truly new and different. It would provide a basis for much planning and change. There would finally be something that parents, pupils and staff could agree or disagree with, and fight to change or alter.

Any such proposal, even if it bore the support of almost everyone, would immediately be attacked as a form of indoctrination and even propaganda. The right of a school or a teacher to make such a claim would be dismissed with the statement: "That is only your opinion." The position of a school is really that it should be absolutely silent in these matters of human happiness, the good life, or description or exemplars of human excellence. Of course, we allow some heroes into our halls but they are almost always fighters for democracy, fighters for the discursive democracy.

We have all been conditioned to think that the discursive democracy model is somehow not a proposal, or not indoctrination. We believe that by not offering pupils a proposal about the good life we allow all sorts of versions of the good life to flourish. In fact, the effect of not proposing any version of the good life on a pupil is from an educational perspective a logical one. The pupil will most likely conclude that unlike electrons, earthquakes and Shakespeare sonnets such a thing as a good life is unlikely to exist.

Our proposal of discursive democracy, devoid of any other value, is in fact indoctrination. Its unfortunate effect is the deadening of a spirit of the ideal in our pupils, and any sense of the necessity to pursue moral excellence rather than to pursue an acceptable democratic consensus of morality. Schools without a proposal for the good life are therefore unlikely to inspire pupils to produce much that is new or exciting or controversial. The school's proposal to pupils is to accept what has been decided as a consensus on almost every issue and to valorise the processes by which such consensus is made. If that sounds engaging and exciting to you, we will have to disagree, in a discursively democratic way, of course.

Chapter 11

SCHOOL REFORM

No Mas

On November 25, 1980, Sugar Ray Leonard faced world champion Roberto Duran in their second boxing match. The first fight, five months previously, had been a classic. That first fight had been a fairly even contest which Duran eventually won. The hyped rematch in New Orleans became famous not for the quality of the contest but for its strange dénouement.

In the eighth round, with Sugar Ray clearly winning the fight, Duran turned his back to his opponent and said No Mas, no more, apparently to the referee. The fight ended inexplicably with the fighter himself giving up towards the end of a round.

Duran was not clearly injured or knocked down when he did this. Speculation from that moment until today about how this hard man who had knocked out a horse with a single punch in a bet to win two bottles of whisky when he was only 14, had suddenly gone "soft", has never abated. The whole culture and ethos of boxing was and is about fighting on, being strong, being a man, hanging in there and never giving up until you are on the canvas, bleeding from multiple gashes or waved off by the referee. Why had this hard man gone so soft so inexplicably quickly?

Duran himself confused matters after the fight and in subsequent decades, giving a variety of explanations from pain in his stomach, to fatigue, to what he loosely termed "frustration". Boxing fans, ignoring as fans always do the commandments of Ockham's razor, began to embroider amazing theories about Duran's uncharacteristic surrender. He quit because he thought he would instantly get a rematch. He quit because of some money deal between managers. He quit because…….

We will never know why Duran said No Mas. He probably does not know himself. My own theory is that he was suddenly struck by the utter futility of what he was doing, a sort of boxing epiphany. In the middle of this huge fight, he caught a whiff of existential ennui.

I always think of Duran when a teacher says No Mas.

We all have felt like Duran and have even said No Mas. In the ring of education, we get to a point where we turn our back to whatever we think the opponent is and whisper No Mas. There are many reasons for this. Teachers and staff can be overwhelmed, over worked, underpaid, and put under stress by careless and thoughtless management directives. Personal circumstances can make the daily battling of teaching too painful. Our own mental health can deteriorate to a point where we cannot go on. Sometimes the reasons for this deterioration are totally unrelated to school.

But I suspect that the need to whisper No Mas is also related to the paradigm of improvement and reform which we use in schools. In just over a decade in our school, I have led a lot of change. Most of my colleagues would say too much change. But on top of the changes to timetables, curricula, calendars, leadership structures, facilities, personnel, programmes, there has been the constant cry of reform.

The word reform describes a process whereby something is declared as faulty, corrupt, erroneous, or useless and then reshaped and relaunched to function again. Reform, so popular with politicians and regulators, therefore, is not just an invitation to change. It carries within it also a condemnation of what has gone before.

I have noticed in my work as a headteacher how painful this can be for the people I work with. There may be perfectly good reasons why change is needed, but reform always implies some failure, some element of brokenness which cannot be fixed. If you work in a school and someone says we have to reform the curriculum, it is impossible not to feel that the curriculum you developed and taught before this sudden announcement and verdict was in some way totally in error. Repeated experiences of being told something you do is completely wrong or needs to be utterly reformed leaves you with two choices. The first is to never invest yourself in what you are doing now as it will likely be declared useless or wrong quite soon and you do not want to emotionally or even intellectually invest in something that is likely to be gone because some person entirely outside of your experience and without consultation with you declares it so. These are the teachers that never really enter the ring but keep a "safe" distance between what they do and what they believe.

The second is to be prepared to be punched in the gut by the experience of negation of your work. It is to put your guard up and your mouthguard in and fight in the ring. It's the people who really care about what they are doing and believe in it who are most hurt by this constant tendency to couch reform in terms of the need to do away with the old, to do away with what people are actually doing. These are the more likely candidates for a Roberto Duran No Mas moment.

Take for example the work that colleagues undertook to master and develop their teaching of certain exam specifications, including coursework components. Suddenly, they find that coursework is no longer deemed valuable. In fact, they are told the reverse. Coursework was an occasion for cheating and added no educational value. Reform means coursework is gone.

If you repeat these sorts of experiences with people who really believe in what they are doing, you create a situation like Duran in that boxing ring. It is not that people are against change. It is that people honestly value their own activity and find it impossible to simply step into a ring to be punched over and over again. A person cannot negate their own intense conviction and commitment. It's quite literally too painful. No Mas.

And where has all the reform of the last decades taken us? I think it is very difficult to prove that reform in its totality has done much to improve education, however we define it, across the UK. We still languish in mediocrity in international comparisons. We still have a horrible attainment gap. There is more illiteracy today than in the 1970s. The self-declared happiness and well- being of young people is not improving and ranks among the lowest in the OECD.

A reasonable person might conclude that it is not schools but reform itself that has failed as a paradigm and a model. Indeed, if madness is defined as continuing to do the same thing and expecting different results, educational reformers should be sectioned.

Different people offer different explanations for why reform does not work in schools. Teachers themselves, allied with left wing politicians, trade unions, and an army of researchers are usually persuaded that an absence of resources, funding and excessive social and economic inequality in society are to blame. I suspect they are at least partially right. However, I find these entirely material and slightly Marxist explanations of what happens in education to be inhuman in themselves. To explain away the failure of reform by insisting that it was never funded properly is in some sense to box with the reformers in their ring on their terms with their own referee. It assumes that given infinite resources even a flawed model of school improvement and change could succeed or that, unless a socialist paradise arises, no school reform will ever succeed.

I have my doubts about this. Fundamentally, the reason reform does not work is because the people implementing the reform say No Mas.

The anthropology and philosophy of school which underpins efforts at reform simply do not take account of the experience of teachers or pupils, and the nature of the educational enterprise itself. Because education touches upon the destiny of the human person and its holistic and complex development, education does not respond well to a reform model which by its definition begins and ends with the elimination of some specific wrong or fault, setting aside the "unreformed" factors.

About a decade ago there was a distinction in US educational research between renewal and reform. Now, we only hear about reform and never about renewal. This is a shame because renewal implies a continuity with the past, a living tradition which is of value and within which solutions can be found, a "bottom up" approach which requires everyone to participate, a desire to engage with the irreducible factor, the human person, in driving change in schools.

This process of renewal is not some new -age fantasy of yoga and crystal rubbing. It can be rigorously and accountably undertaken. It can even have the key performance indicators so beloved of managers. A simple way to phrase the challenge of renewal is to ask: "How can we change an outcome by changing our view of and approach to what are doing rather than changing what we are doing?" Such an invitation is the opposite of being punched in a boxing ring. It asks a person to reflect, to create, to change the gaze with which they look upon their current practice and all its assumptions. Such an approach sometimes leads to much more fundamental change than even a reformer thought possible because it is obvious that a different gaze leads to a different approach which in turn leads to a different practice. In fact, renewal allows people to take down the ropes of the ring and shout Mas! Mas!

Epilogue

Lockdown is already triggering proposals and plans for the complete reimagining of education. Many of these proposals focus on on-line learning and solving, as ever, the problem of unequal outcomes.

If lockdown has taught anything other than the pure contingency of our existence, it is the fact that we are social and material creatures. We miss the community that is school, the chance to see each other, and to share our days together. I am not sure on-line learning is the answer to our educational discontent even if we can all admire the heroic and effective efforts of teachers during the crisis to teach remotely. Certainly, the lockdown has shown conclusively that parents are the most important educators in any child's life and that the culture of the home can be very conducive to academic learning or destructive of it.

Unequal and unfair educational outcomes will be exacerbated by this hiatus in school life. It has become apparent that schools with buildings, teachers, and people in them are a necessary ingredient for the safety and learning of some children. Zoom will not do. Relationships develop when we are in the same place together.

For me, lockdown has inspired reflection on the mystery that is school. The ingredients of that mystery are the persons who make up school. Lockdown has returned me again and again to the need to place the person with all of his or her desires, needs and reasons at the centre of the school. Persons cannot be manipulated, contained or understood in any reduced paradigm of the human experience. The freedom of the person is the real test of an education. How to engage that freedom is a noble but also fiendishly difficult task. Beethoven said: "Art! Who comprehends her? With whom can one consult concerning this great goddess?" I ask the same question about the school I lead and find that I too am looking for a someone or something to consult with about this mystery.

In lockdown, inspired by a renewed acquaintance with my faith in the form of the writings of a Milanese Religious Studies teacher, I have become persuaded that schools should seek to introduce pupils as persons to an expanded use of their reason as it relates to all of reality and to apply that reason to the totality of experience, including matters which are deemed ineffable and unverifiable through measurement. I believe that pupils as persons should be presented with a clear proposal about the meaning of this totality of reality and encouraged to test and verify that proposal by the light of their own experience. I believe that we should invite our pupils to consider their time at school as an apprenticeship for working on the world, whose primary means is the development of a mature concept of human freedom.

I have no plan to bring any of these things about. Ruminations are not programmes. I trust that our consultation and reflection about this mystery called school will lead to renewed expressions and communication of our deepest hopes and desires.

Plans, if desired, will come after that.

About the Author

Hans has studied, taught and led schools in the US and the UK. He is a native of the Netherlands. He is currently the principal of Liverpool College, an academy school for pupils aged 4-19. He lives with his family in Liverpool.

Printed in Great Britain
by Amazon